BROKEN
DESTINY

THE STORY OF SERGEANT WILLIAM M. O'LOUGHLIN,
UNITED STATES ARMY AIR FORCE

MARK VERWIEL
&
MARIO ACEVEDO

For all war Veterans and their families that suffered the loss of a loved one who was willing to pay the ultimate price for their country.

and

For the entire Verwiel/O'Loughlin/Murphy and Ladwig Families.

*"No one is actually dead until the ripples they cause
in the world die away"*
- Terry Pratchett, British Author

Prologue

Everyone has a story to tell of successes and failures, triumphs and tragedies, amidst the everyday parts of our lives. Some stories are told over and over again, whereas others are lost to time or suppressed because of the pain involved in remembering them. This is the story of a forgotten man, my great Uncle Bill, whose memory had been packed away by my family for decades, then brought to life by a series of strange coincidences and unlikely events. These incidents kept bringing his story back to the surface until this book came together.

The sorrow from the loss of Uncle Bill in 1944 radiated through our family, stoking a grief so profound that it was necessary to stow away his wartime death. But in so doing so, this prevented the memory of his service and sacrifice from being passed on to the next generations, including my own.

My interest in Uncle Bill's story began with a simple question, "Who is this?" And thereafter, it was as if Uncle Bill decided to drop bread crumbs from the spiritual world to encourage me to continue my pursuit. Scoff at the unlikely interventions all you want, but had they not occurred, this book would have never been written.

This story is a glimpse into history, told through the life of a man largely forgotten for many decades. This telling opens a portal to a past quickly receding, of a man, my father's uncle—William Maurice O'Loughlin—swept up by a world war that destroyed nations, obliterated millions and with them, many of their stories. I hope this narrative will bring back to life not only Uncle Bill and his fellow airmen, but also the travails of his young wife and their extended family back on the home front.

January 2, 2000

I thought 1999 was a bad year. On Christmas Eve, my father suffered a massive heart attack. Unfortunately, the new millennium brought a second heart attack, even worse than the first. Our family took turns staying with my dad as he convalesced at home.

While with him during the second week of January, I rummaged through a pile of magazines and books on his living room coffee table to find a photo album my aunts, his sisters, had put together as a Christmas present for their siblings—all twelve of them. While flipping through the pages, to my surprise I discovered a photo of a dark-haired stranger in military uniform who bore an uncanny resemblance to my dad's family. It was a clipping from a Chicago newspaper announcing that he (and several other local men) had been determined to be missing or killed in action in January 1944. Apparently, this was standard fare for newspapers of that time.

"Who is this?" I asked my dad.

"That is my Uncle Bill," my father replied with a sigh. "William O'Loughlin. He was killed fighting in Italy during World War II. I don't know much about the story of how he died, but I do remember that he was the life of the family. I was about seven years old when he was killed. I can still hear my grandmother's cries from the apartment above ours when a phone call came to the house. Still sends a shiver up my spine."

This revelation astonished me. This was the first I'd heard that a family member had fought in that war, much less that he had died in combat. I had recently been indulging a growing interest in World War II, having read many books about the war. I studied the photo; it was a classic snapshot from the period, a moment captured in the black and white we've come to associate with that era.

"How come no one ever talked about him?"

"His death brought a lot of grief to my mother, my grandmother, and his other siblings. For obvious reasons, it was especially hard on Aunt Betty who was married to Bill for little more than a year. They had a daughter named Maureen. His death broke Betty's heart. It was easier not to talk about it than dwell on the tragedy. After a while, we stopped talking about him."

My dad's explanation filled in the blanks to questions I never knew existed. I didn't know anything about Betty and Maureen as I was removed from them by two generations. But I felt a nudging that there was more that needed to be answered. A door into our past had cracked open, and it invited me to enter and explore.

In the ensuing weeks I couldn't get this William Maurice O'Loughlin—Uncle Bill—out of my mind. At the suggestion of a work friend (Christian), I wrote to the federal government for information they might have regarding Bill. Months later, their replies trickled back: mostly photocopies of correspondence between the government and Bill's wife, Betty, and his mother, Florence. She really just wanted to know what had happened to her son. Most intriguing was a photocopy of a listing of the contents of Bill's footlocker the day of his death: some letters, a photo of Betty, a broken rosary, a prayer book, spare change, and a comb. Nothing scandalous and it seemed about right considering the staunch Catholic upbringing of my family. However, after staring at the correspondence, I couldn't help but be struck with an empty feeling of, "So that's it? This guy's legacy is summed up in a few painful letters and a list of trinkets he left behind?"

After my dad's heart attack, every member of my family rallied around him in order to keep him busy and active. He couldn't run his consulting business anymore and his physical abilities were somewhat limited.

Two activities, however, kept my father and me connected.

First, I started refurbishing old British sports cars like Triumphs and Jaguars, which he had worked on when I was a kid. We could talk for hours about these cars, how there was always something that needed fixing and yet, how they were some of the most beautiful automobiles ever built. We even went in together on a Jaguar that allowed him to restart his hobby.

The second activity was our continued interest in Uncle Bill. We continued researching wherever possible for more information about his wartime service. Gradually, the records we received made for an intriguing trove of information that I collected in a special folder.

Page by page, detail by detail, Uncle Bill began to emerge from the hazy recesses of history. The more I learned about him, those black-and-white images filled with color and he was transformed from an abstract memory into a man who had lived and loved among us.

My father traveled to Alabama to visit Bill's daughter, Maureen, and learn what he could about her father. My mother helped with this project as she was interested in genealogy and even offered to help finance the writing of whatever came from this effort, hopefully Uncle Bill's biography.

My dad was a part-time fiction writer, and we decided he should complete this work on Uncle Bill. In 2014, my dad moved down the street from me, and then we bought a boat together. He was intrigued by the romance of living on a boat, writing another book, and watching the goings-on of the harbor's transient setting. It was a good couple of years for him, but in 2017 his fumbling heart caught up with him.

At first I thought the effort for this book would fade with my dad's passing, but then a series of odd events convinced me that I would not rest until this story was completed.

As an archetype in storytelling, there is the journey of the reluctant hero. While I don't consider myself at all heroic, events beyond my control compelled me to finish this journey and answer the question, *Who was William Maurice O'Loughlin?*

1

Friday, December 31, 1943, Amendola, Italy

The new year could've started much better for Sergeant William Maurice O'Loughlin.

Last night, O'Loughlin had finished the last morsel of the fruit cake his wife Betty had sent him. Anything from home was always a treat and a welcome diversion from mess hall chow. He had gone to bed reflecting over her letter and what he would write to her.

Sometime before dawn, a fierce Italian winter storm ravaged the unit's encampment. Cyclone-like winds flattened tents. Men hollered and cursed. Sheets of freezing rain poured upon the hapless soldiers, now exposed to the bitter elements.

O'Loughlin lay on his cot, still warm and dry in his sleeping bag, giving himself a moment before deciding to rush outside to help his comrades. "All right," he shouted to his tentmates, "everybody out of the sack and give a hand." He pulled on his trousers and field jacket and hurriedly jammed his bare feet into his boots.

Two tent stakes ripped from the ground and the violent shaking of their tent threatened to knock over the support poles. O'Loughlin and his buddies dashed to limit the damage. In a panicked rush, their first priority was to secure the tent's kerosene stove and keep it from spilling fuel that would have set the tent and their bedding on fire.

That accomplished, while the other men held the poles upright from underneath the wet canvas, O'Loughlin and Sergeant Leo Hassett ventured outside to re-anchor the stakes. This was no easy feat as the wind batted the tent about. The loose canvas slapped wildly and made the guide ropes lash at their faces like frenzied whips while the cold rain soaked through their uniforms.

Hassett positioned a corner stake and O'Loughlin hammered it with a wooden mallet. When the stake had been firmly planted, O'Loughlin grabbed a guide rope and tied it into place. The wind continued to buffet the tent, making the guide rope twist against the stake. O'Loughlin worried the stake might yank free but it held.

Before they started on the next stake, he took measure of the chaos around him. Few of the tents had been spared. Men just as wet and woebegone as he was struggled to contain their personal catastrophes. The tents belonging to Operations and Communications lay in wadded heaps, water pooling on the canvas. Desks, tables, and typewriters were strewn about. File cabinets had toppled onto their sides, the drawers gaping open. The unrelenting wind drove sheets of paper—from those reports so beloved by the military bureaucracy—over the muddy ground.

The rain let up enough for O'Loughlin to scope out the airfield. To the east, the rising sun brought a dim, gray light to the landscape. In the distance, blurred by mist, stood the squadron's B-25 bombers. The large airplanes with their crooked wings resembled sleeping dragons hunkered down to wait out the storm. Empty, the bombers weighed almost nine tons and as heavy as they were, the big airplanes rocked and strained against the ropes anchoring them to the ground.

A sheet of rain sprayed over O'Loughlin. Icy water coursed down his neck, along his back, chilling him to his bones. His footing slipped in the cold slop puddled around the tent and freezing, gritty mud splashed inside his boots, adding to his discomfort.

The frigid temperatures turned his hands into painful hooks that made it a challenge to hold onto the slick, wet tent fabric as the howling wind tried to wrestle it from his grasp. O'Loughlin couldn't remember a time when he'd been this miserable.

As he struggled to hold onto the canvas, he thought about the news Betty had written about her sister Shirley. How she was engaged to some new guy . . . a Doctor Wall. A dentist and a 4F possibly! At the time, not knowing anything about him, O'Loughlin imagined he was some cavity filler who thought himself too precious to do his part for the war. And by do his part, that meant, get his goldbricking ass in uniform and going wherever the hell Uncle Sam sent him. Like here for starters.

The idea brought a bit of humor and lightened his mood.

"Hey Leo," he shouted to Hassett, "just think. If it wasn't for the army, we wouldn't be enjoying ourselves in beautiful sunny Italy."

Sergeant William Maurice O'Loughlin belonged to the 447th Bomber Squadron, 321st Bombardment Group, of the 57th Bombardment Wing, comprised mainly of medium bombers, three groups of B-25 Mitchells and three groups of B-26 Marauders. These planes were key elements within the 12th Air Force, tasked with providing air support for the Allied offensive that drove the Nazis out of north Africa, across the Mediterranean, and now up the Italian boot.

Aboard the B-25, O'Loughlin served as its flight engineer. Those duties included helping the pilot and co-pilot monitor the engine instruments when airborne. Before operations, he honchoed over the ground crew to make sure that his airplane was mission ready. In combat though, his responsibilities took on a more aggressive role as he had to man the tail stinger—a single .50 caliber machine gun mounted in a Plexiglas cone.

Like many of his fellow crewmen who served by the hundreds of thousands either on ships or on lands far away from home, in idle moments O'Loughlin's thoughts tended to wander to what, or rather who, he had left behind. In this case, it was his wife Betty, formerly Ruth Elizabeth Cummings, now Mrs. Ruth Betty O'Loughlin, who he had married in August, 1942. They didn't have much of a honeymoon but the short time they had together before shipping out seemed productive enough.

Which was confirmed in late August when he received a V-Mail letter from Betty. On the 19th of the month, she had given birth to their daughter, Maureen. William Maurice O'Loughlin was now a father. Now he had two important reasons to return home safe and whole.

By eight in the morning the tent was up and secure though the storm remained as savage as before. O'Loughlin and his tentmates took turns sweeping water and mud off the wooden planks arranged as flooring. Hassett brewed a pot of coffee on the tent stove. The men strung cord around the tent to hang wet clothes and bedding to dry.

O'Loughlin changed into his driest uniform and relaxed on his cot to enjoy a welcome cup of coffee and a respite from this damnable weather. No doubt, breakfast chow would be late.

He lit a cigarette and enjoyed how the warm smoke and the warm coffee coursed through him and brought to mind warm thoughts. He found himself smiling.

"God, I hate this," Schrader grumbled as he wrung a wet sock. "O'Loughlin, what keeps you in such good spirits?"

O'Loughlin regarded his two companions. "Thinking about home. My wife, Betty. My daughter, Maureen."

He placed a fresh V-Mail stationery page on a clipboard and sat on the edge of his cot to write:

Hi Sweetheart,

I received two packages from you today, hon! They were very nice and I got a lot of pleasure out of opening them up. Everything was lovely darling and we got rid of that fruit cake in a hurry.

So Shirley is now engaged. Just when did this Dr. Wall come into the picture? What is he, another 4F? If he isn't why isn't he in the army? I'm sure they can use another dentist. Perhaps, I'm prejudiced but I knew and liked Al and don't like the idea of a slacker making hay while he is away. Of course, it's none of my business and Al might never have had a chance but I still don't like the idea.

Well, there is no sense in my getting up over it because there is no telling how I might go once and get a good start. Time enough for that once I get home but that certain people will know just how I feel the first time we meet. I was sorry to hear you had such a nasty pneumonia. You take more care of yourself hon. Those pictures Pat took also arrived today and I liked them a lot. They are the first nice pictures I had of you and the baby, darling. She looks cute as the dickens by me. Oh my!! How I would love to see her. Well, say its New Year's Eve now darling.

Love, Bill

2

William "Bill" Maurice O'Loughlin was born 1918, though some records mention 1919. Much about Bill's early days has been lost in the mists of history. What is certain was that he was the third child and the only son born to Florence O'Loughlin, whose maiden name was Hickey.

Bill was named after his father, William O'Loughlin, who passed away in 1931 at the age of 55. While Bill's father's premature death created hardship for his widow, he had fortunately provided her with a pension that helped ease her financial burdens as a single mother during the Depression. Even so, the household budget remained a strain, and Bill decided that the family was better off if he worked rather than stay in school.

Tuesday, March 12, 1940

Bill drove the McCloud Candy Company delivery van along Chicago's East 79th Street. His best friend Carl Ladwig leaned against the passenger's side door of the Dodge's cab.

"Too bad there's us both in the truck," Bill said. "The old man is getting two for the price of one."

"It's either that, or no work at all," Carl replied. "You ever think of that?"

"All the time. The newspapers are telling us that sunny times are here again but I'm not feeling it."

"So what are you going to do?" Carl asked.

Bill shrugged. "I'm still trying to figure that out."

"Go back to school?" Carl asked.

"Naw. I hate school. My dad wanted me to be a building engineer like him."

"It was a good job."

"But not for me." Bill waved to the tall buildings around them. "There's a big world out there and I can't see myself trapped in a basement fussing with boilers and the plumbing. I'd have to go back to school and then college."

"And?"

"Why learn about stuff I'll never use? It's a waste of my time."

"Then what?" Carl asked.

"Like I said. I'm still trying to figure that out." Bill pressed the clutch. "We're coming up on Sander's Drugstore."

Carl picked up a cardboard box filled with boxes of *Oh Henry, Baby Ruth, Carmies,* and *Red Hots.* He double-checked the invoice. Bill eased the van beside the cars already parked along the curb. The instant he stopped, the car on his rear bumper began honking. Delivery in hand, Carl sprang out. Cool spring air burst into the cab. The car honked again. Bill looked into the rearview mirror and saw the driver shaking his fist.

Bill waved back. "Same to you, buddy." He proceeded down the street and turned right to circle the block. Part of the strategy of having two men in the truck was to speed deliveries. One of them hopped out to make the delivery while the other kept circling. This was a work-around to Chicago's notorious parking challenges.

When Bill returned to Sander's Drugstore, Carl was waiting at the curb. Bill slowed only enough for Carl to leap on board. He slapped an envelope against the back of Bill's head. "Delivery made. Invoice paid."

As they proceeded to their next stop, Bill read bills posted to the passing walls. Considering this was Chicago, most were familiar political rants, but it was the newest of the bills that caught his attention. It was red and blue on white paper that proclaimed: *America First! No War for us in Europe!*

Bill panned the bill, then returned his gaze to traffic. "Whaddaya think?"

Carl had also noticed the bill. "A war? I hope not."

Bill understood. All of his life he'd tried not to stare at the aging Civil War veterans, most of whom had an empty sleeve or trouser leg gathered and pinned. Then there were the many veterans of the First World War—broken, homeless men his father's age.

But there was no denying that world events were boiling over. You'd have to be blind and deaf to not know that the British and the French were brawling with the Germans—*again!*—for control of western Europe. And the Japanese were doing some mischief in China.

The America Firsters claimed that the US had already shed enough blood in the First World War, and that it was in our interests to keep out. Then there was the opposing view that the Nazis were no friends of America and sooner or later, our two countries would come to blows. Problem was, the Nazi-haters were armchair intellectuals, too old and too privileged to fight themselves.

Carl must've been thinking the same thing because he said, "If America gets into the war, it's gonna be up to guys like me and you to do the fighting."

Bill nudged the steering wheel, not certain of his part in history. He barely managed his own affairs, much less those of the whole world. *Then again,* he reminded himself, *ah hell,… I always get things to turn my way.*

After work, Bill returned to his mother's apartment on the second floor of their apartment building on 72nd Place. When he opened the door to the family apartment, he smelled pasta cooking. Stepping inside, he made a face at his youngest sister, Patricia, who responded by rolling her eyes.

His mother was in the kitchen chopping carrots while his older sister, Florence, was busy making dinner: spaghetti casserole with white sauce. Bill looked at the dish and wrinkled his nose.

His mother dumped the chopped carrots into the casserole. "What's the matter?"

"Gee mom, after a man works a hard day like I have, he looks forward to a good meal." Bill made an exaggerated display of placing a dollar bill on the table.

"A whole dollar!" Florence snorted. "I made that much today at Goodson's Market and you don't see me acting like I'm too good for this." She tapped a mixing spoon against the casserole dish.

Bill hooked his fingers into the waistband of his trousers and rocked on his heels. "But you haven't been risking life and limb like I have on the mean streets of Chicago. It's a jungle out there."

Florence rolled her eyes. "Spare me, Lord Fauntleroy."

His mother opened the icebox. "I have steak." She pointed to the pantry cabinet. "A can of green beans? Toast?"

"That works. I'll be ready in about twenty minutes."

"Where are you going?" Florence asked.

"Meeting with Carl. We're taking in a movie. *Remember the Night.*"

She abruptly rinsed her hands in the sink and pulled off her apron. "Mom, I'm going."

Bill knew his sister was sweet on Carl, which was okay because Bill liked him as well. Whether or not things between Florence and Carl got serious, that was not something Bill would worry about.

"What about the casserole?" their mom asked.

Florence shoved the dish into the oven and glanced at the wall clock. "When I'm ready, it'll be done." She rushed to her bedroom.

Patricia had been watching. She asked, "Why does Bill get steak and the rest of us get casserole?"

Bill tousled her hair. "Remember, I'm the man of the house."

She swung around to swat him. Bill dodged the blow and headed into his bedroom to collect his change of clothes. He retreated into the bathroom and emerged in fresh clothes, smelling clean, his hair neatly parted and pomaded into place. His steak was ready and he sat to eat.

Florence took his place in the bathroom. He heard the tap run, then squeak off. In a loud voice he warned, "I'll be leaving without you, ready or not."

He asked his mom. "Where's Eileen?" She was the sibling born after him and the sister he had the most in common with.

"She hasn't returned from work," his mom replied. "Still out with friends." Eileen was as free-spirited as Bill and that was why they were so close.

The bathroom door flung open. Clad in a housecoat, Florence hustled toward her bedroom, mumbling, "I'm hurrying. I'm hurrying."

Bill ate his steak at a casual pace and sopped his plate with the toast. He enjoyed being the man of the house.

Bill's mother was mending dresses by her bedroom window, where the light was best for this precise work. With her late-husband's pension and with what Florence, Bill, and Eileen contributed to the household budget, the family was comfortable. Still, she cut corners whenever she could; sewing up rips and updating clothes stretched the family dollars. The oldest of her brood, Marcelline, had married John Verwiel and already started a family of their own.

I'm a grandmother, how did that happen? Bill's mom mused when she heard the apartment door click open. She listened and could tell it was Bill. This was the middle of the afternoon and he should be at work. What happened? Normally, his steps were quick and lively. This time they sounded heavy and troubled.

She put the needle and thread aside and left the bedroom. Bill hung his suit coat on a wall peg and proceeded to the sofa where he sat, stiff and pondering. She studied his expression, deciding that he was brooding rather than being in a serious jam.

He sat with his hands anchored on the knees of his gangly legs. When he looked in her direction it seemed as though he was looking through her and not at her. His gaze was distant and cool rather than his usual charming and warm.

She knew that it was easier to pry open an oyster with your fingers than it was to get Bill to talk about what bothered him. She decided to do what she always did. Fuss over him until he decided to share what was on his mind.

"Would you like tea?"

"Too hot," he said simply.

"Iced sugar water with lemon?"

When he was in one of these moods, if he didn't answer, that meant yes.

When she returned with the drink, he took it, sipped, and rested the glass on one knee. "I've made a decision."

She waited for him to elaborate.

Which he did. In a way when he said, "I have to leave."

She felt a stab of remorse but tried to not let it show. "Where? Why?"

He smiled, his charm returning. "Let me surprise you. Nothing bad. It's that I need direction in my life. I have to feel as though I'm making a difference."

He was twenty-two and still living at home and working one dead-end job after another. But what kind of a change was he contemplating?

"Don't you worry, Mother. I won't be gone long. And when I return, things will be different."

She wanted to ask, *Different how? Can't we talk about this?* But Bill, being Bill, wouldn't talk about it. As always, he knew what was best for Bill.

The next day, he vanished.

In August, a post card from Bill arrived at his mother's home. The front image was a photograph of a business street crowded with cars, a scene that could've been anywhere. On the back, Bill had scrawled:

> *Miss you all. Am doing great.*
> *See you soon.*
> *Love,*
> *Bill*

The only clue about his whereabouts was the postmark. Oklahoma City. *What was in Oklahoma?*

She studied the postcard and worried about what Bill had done. He was impulsive, a bit reckless, but never foolish. *Where was he? What was he doing?*

Marcelline "Pudy" Verwiel was the first child of Marcelline (Marce), Bill's oldest sister, and her husband John Verwiel.

Pudy was on the back porch of her apartment building, which overlooked a small backyard enclosed by a tall fence.

Movement in the alley caught her eye. A hand appeared over the gate, fumbling for the latch. *What's going on?* she thought. People didn't come into the backyard unless they lived in the building. Visitors were supposed to enter the building at the front vestibule and ring the bell over the correct mailbox to be buzzed in. She stood and watched, not so much alarmed as curious.

The gate swung open and through it, sauntered her Uncle Bill. He wore a military uniform—olive drab with brass buttons, and a khaki shirt with a matching tie. The insignia on his lapels sparkled like jewelry. In one hand he carried an army-issue leather travel bag.

She was about to exclaim, "Uncle Bill!" when he put a finger to his lips. She covered her mouth to keep from shouting. Knowing that the family worried about him, and giddy with happiness, she bounced on her feet.

Bill crossed the yard in an easy, loping stride, and bounded up the stairs. He picked her up and gave a big hug, which she returned. She was crazy about her fun-loving, always teasing, Uncle Bill.

"Where have you been?" she asked.

"Far away. Doing things."

"What kind of things?"

"Army things."

Bill set her down, and again put a finger to his lips. "Shhhh."

Thrilled to see him and excited to be part of his secret, Pudy kept quiet. He hustled up the stairs to the second floor and she chased after him. He reached the door to his mother's apartment and gave one loud knock. Pudy waited behind him.

Footfalls approached the door. It was his sister Eileen who answered.

Bill shouted, "Surprise!"

Eileen's eyes widened. "Bill!"

There was a chaotic scramble to the door, the homey atmosphere yielding to shrieks of joy, peals of laughter, a volley of questions.

"Bill?"

"You're in a uniform."

"Where have you been?"

Eileen and his youngest sister Patricia pulled him inside. Pudy turned about and rushed to her apartment, flinging the door open and yelling, "Mom! Dad! Uncle Bill is back!"

Marcelline and John race up the stairs to join in the excitement and celebrations. Everyone crowded into the kitchen, a happy bedlam of questions and hugs.

Florence, Bill's mother, motioned toward the living room. "Grammy needs to sit down."

Once in the living room, the buzz of conversation quieted. However, everyone looked at Bill for answers. He grinned, definitely enjoying the moment and the excitement.

"OK," he began dramatically. "The news is," he took a deep breath, "I've joined the Illinois National Guard." He paused a beat. "I'm in the artillery."

A shocked voice from somewhere in the room asked, "You're in the Illinois National Guard artillery?"

"Yep, that's where I've been. In Fort Sill, Oklahoma. For basic training and artillery school."

The mood grew tense as war was on everyone's mind.

Sensing the grimness, Bill explained, "We all know things in Europe are bad. Sooner or later, it will come to us. We need to be prepared for when war does come to us."

His brother-in-law, John Verwiel stepped forward, smiling, and shook Bill's hand. "Oh, you O'Loughlins! Always ready for a fight. And you go signing up like you can't wait."

3

March 1941

Bill paced alongside his sisters, Florence and Eileen, as the two women walked arm-in-arm. The evening spring air brimmed with the possibilities of spontaneous fun. They were in downtown Chicago and on the way to meet Carl Ladwig for a night at the movies.

Florence nudged Bill. "Can I tell you something people have been saying about you?"

"You know I'm not one for gossip," he replied. They continued for several steps when he tugged at her elbow. "Well, go on."

She deflected her gaze from the path ahead to him. "It's your uniform. It's changed you."

"I don't think so."

"I mean, before you joined the army, you seemed kinda lost."

"I'll admit, I was looking for purpose."

"Maybe you found it," she remarked. "The uniform does make you look good."

"It's the other way around," he said dryly. "You mean I make the uniform look good."

His reply was so typically Bill. Florence thought that he was always careful with his appearance; now he fussed constantly with his uniform. He wouldn't leave the house unless the uniform's creases were sharp, though it was their mom who ironed the shirt and trousers. Last thing before bed, he made sure his shoes were mirror shiny. Before he put on his uniform, Bill removed the brass insignia to polish each piece then carefully positioning them just so on the coat lapel. He made it a point to grasp his service cap in a certain way so he wouldn't smudge the brim, and he carried a kerchief to wipe fingerprints from his brass belt buckle. Florence hadn't realized that a military uniform required so much bother.

Bill wore a single stripe on his upper sleeve, meaning he had the rank of Private First Class. Florence knew that this was the next to the lowest rank, but that didn't keep Bill from strutting about like Napoleon. Kids on the street would run up to him, stand rigid, and salute. Sometimes older men would tease by calling him, "General."

Regardless, Bill seemed to enjoy the attention.

Up ahead, the line in front of the theater parted enough for them to see Carl Ladwig. Eileen wandered off as she was to meet other friends. Since Carl hadn't yet decided to join the army, he wore an ordinary suit, set off with a colorful tie.

Bill grasped Florence by the arm. "Look what I found wandering the streets."

She gave Bill a playful slap then extended her hand for Carl.

"You hang on to that one," Bill said. "I already got my other sister Marce out of the house. Fewer sisters at home means more steak for me."

They bought tickets for Errol Flynn's newest offering, *The Sea Hawk*. In the lobby, Bill detoured to the concession stand. He was browsing the candy counter when he spotted a pretty blonde behind the counter. She appeared in her early twenties—about Bill's age—and wore a white apron over a pale-yellow dress. Her only makeup was red lipstick, which meant she was confident enough with her looks that she didn't need to slather on foundation or rouge. They made eye contact and she slid toward him.

"Anything I can help you with?"

Bill smiled. "I'm not sure. I was in the mood for candy and now I'm in the mood for something else."

She gestured to the soda fountain. "Maybe you're thirsty?"

An usher announced, "The movie is about to start."

Bill's mind sputtered with indecision. "I better take my seat. I'll be back. Yes?"

She smiled. "You know where to find me."

Bill hustled into the theater. Florence waved from a middle row where she sat with Carl. Bill rushed to an empty seat beside his sister.

The movie was preceded by a *Movietones* newsreel that depicted the tragedy unfolding in Europe. All manner of war machines paraded across the screen—submarines attacking ships, ships attacking submarines, tanks tearing through villages, and lots of airplanes buzzing above ruined landscapes. Florence studied Bill to see how he took it all in. The light flickered on his face, highlighting his handsome features, but his expression remained placid, giving no hint of any misgivings about his potential role should war come to America.

During the feature, Bill, like everyone else in the theater, laughed at the jokes, gasped at the thrilling parts, and sighed impatiently during the maudlin, melodramatic moments.

When the final credits began, Bill rushed from his seat and side-stepped his way through the growing crowd toward the lobby. He searched the concession stand and the blonde he'd been talking to was gone. He approached a teenage boy filling bags of popcorn.

"Have you seen the blonde working the stand?"

The boy turned and looked at Bill. "Which blonde? We got three, maybe four."

"The pretty one."

The boy grinned. "They're all pretty. You got a name?"

Bill exhaled in frustration. He cursed himself for not asking her.

Florence strode by and corralled him. They headed to Gerald's Malt Shop, where they were lucky to find an empty booth on such a busy Thursday night. Florence sat beside Carl while Bill sat opposite. They ordered Cokes and a plate of French fries.

Then, from the corner of his eye, Bill spotted the blonde from the theater concession stand. She was sitting at the counter, appearing quite fashionable with a beige tweed jacket over her dress. Bill excused himself, slid from the booth, and sauntered toward the comely young woman.

Bill leaned ever so slightly toward her. His confidence and charisma brightened several notches. "Remember me?"

"Of course. I waited for you."

He shrugged, then grinned. "But I'm here now. Are you by yourself?"

She met his gaze, her eyes as lively as his. "Actually, I'm here with friends."

The two women on her left waved.

Bill gestured to the empty space at his booth. "That's more comfortable. Plus you get to sit next to me."

"Is that right?" she chuckled. "Won't your friends object?"

"Actually, they're not my friends. The gal is my sister and the guy next to her is some goofball she picked up off the street."

Florence and Carl waved.

The woman gave Bill the once-over. "I've never dated a man in uniform."

He beamed. "So we're dating? My, you move fast."

"Like I suppose you're a slow poke when it comes to girls."

"I'm not a slow poke at anything. The name is Bill O'Loughlin."

"Betty Cummings."

She slid off the counter stool and to her friends, mimed talking on a phone. "I'll fill you in later."

Florence and Betty got along immediately. As they all picked at the plate of fries and sipped at their drinks, the conversation swirled around the booth, never sagging into an awkward pause. Turns out that Betty lived close to the O'Loughlin's apartment, which made Bill wonder why he'd never seen her before. Maybe he had? But he felt sure he'd have remembered this pretty lady.

When it was time to go, they all four strolled in the same direction, Carl and Florence arm-in-arm, Bill and Betty trailing behind. Bill slowed his steps to increase the distance between them and Florence, since his sister had a habit of making his business her business.

As the two couples walked down the street, their shadows shrank and elongated when they passed beneath the street lights. The night air was pleasant and cool, perfect weather for strolling at a leisurely pace.

Betty was pretty, fetching actually, and Bill felt the more he talked to her, the more he liked her.

"What do you like to do?" he asked. "I mean what are you good at?"

"I sing choir and play the piano."

You don't say?" he asked. "So do I."

"That's wonderful," she replied, excited. "Maybe we could practice a duet."

"Whoa. Whoa," he protested. "I said I can sing and play the piano. I never said I was any good."

She laughed and punched his arm. "So what are you good at?"

Bill scrunched his face in feigned concentration. "Lessee. Watching movies."

She nodded. "So am I. We have that in common."

Up ahead, Carl and Florence paused and looked back at Bill and Betty. They had reached the street for the O'Loughlin home.

Bill said to Betty, "I'm going to walk you home, if it's okay."

Her cheeks dimpled. "I was hoping on it." She guided him by the arm so they continued straight. Bill waved to Florence that she and Carl should go on without them.

"What are your plans?" Betty asked, her tone getting serious. "For life, I mean."

He steered her around a patch of broken pavement. "I dunno. Meet some pretty girl. You know any?"

She punched him again. "I'm serious? Can you be serious for just a minute or two?"

"I tried once. And a disaster happened."

"Really? What?"

"I met some gal named Betty."

"Another Betty? What was she like—" Betty paused in mid-step. She recovered and swung her hand at Bill.

It was midnight when Bill returned to his mom's apartment. He hooked his service cap on a coat rack and carefully slipped his uniform coat onto a wooden hanger. He moved slowly, deliberately, as if he was aware that his life had changed, perhaps more so than when he had joined the National Guard. Earlier this evening when he'd stepped out with his sister Florence, she was on a date with Carl, and Bill was stag. That didn't bother him at the time because he knew that sooner or later he'd meet someone. There were no shortages of available girls in the world.

Then he met Betty and suddenly he wasn't interested in any other girls, and this realization kindled a heat within him, a warmth of promise and fulfillment that he'd never known before.

His mother, Florence, and sister, Pat, were at the kitchen table, the three of them highlighted by the yellow circle of illumination from the ceiling bulb. A teapot sat on the table but only their mom had poured herself a cup.

Bill loosened his tie and unbuttoned his top collar button.

Pat raised an eyebrow. "What's gotten into you?"

Bill pulled a chair from the table and folded his lanky frame onto the seat. What he said next simply spilled out of his mouth, "I just met the woman I'm going to marry."

July 12, 1941

When Bill heard that Carl was going to tie the knot with Florence, he put in for a furlough to attend the wedding, which was granted. The mood in the army was one of muted anxiety. No one knew when the actual shooting would start, nor where, or under what conditions. Until then, the attitude was one of wait and see and soldiers were allowed liberal time off, well aware that when the war came to America, then routines and travel would be locked tight.

At the moment, Bill stood next to Carl, outside St. Laurence Catholic Church. As best man, Bill wore a tweed double-breasted suit. Carl wore a white blazer over black trousers, both puffed on cigarettes. They were facing Betty who aimed the camera. The day was decidedly pleasant, perfect in fact, and she wore a loose, pale yellow dress with a matching hat.

Bill reflected on the passing of time and the way that outwardly, much had changed in their lives, though inwardly, he still regarded Carl as fondly as when they first met as boys. Now as grown men, they were still best friends.

After the photo, Bill beckoned for Betty to stand beside him for their picture. Florence took the camera and Carl watched over her shoulder. Bill lit a cigarette and waited for the shot.

"Betty," Carl said, "it's not too late to find another fella."

Bill snorted. "Hey Carl, the last time I saw a face like yours it was at the zoo."

"Hush you two," Florence said. She squinted through the viewfinder. "Okay, Bill, Betty, say cheese."

Betty grabbed the cigarette from Bill's fingers and dropped it on the grass. She leaned into Bill and they both said, "Cheese."

The next day, after a day on the town, Bill accompanied Betty to her apartment. He'd worn his uniform, which brought them many admiring looks. On the way there, he'd picked up a bouquet of flowers from a corner market.

They had spent the day chatting about many things but throughout the day, Betty felt the passing of time as a tangible experience, like she was in an hourglass with the sand shifting beneath her feet. She was appreciative that Bill had bought the flowers as they lifted her mood. Once in her apartment, she put them in a vase and placed it on an end table.

He made his way to the sofa. She sat beside him. He placed his hat on the coffee table and reached inside his uniform coat. "I got something to show you." He withdrew an envelope. Inside were snapshots. He displayed one of him aiming a revolver.

"Meant to show these earlier. This is me doing marksmanship training. I'm a pretty good shot."

Betty frowned. She wanted to talk about something else besides war matters. The only question she could manage was, "They let you keep the gun?"

"I wish. But no. We have to turn in our weapons at the end of the day unless we're on guard duty."

Bill showed her the remaining pictures of him and his buddies standing outside barracks or in front of army trucks. She did her best to pay attention to what he was explaining, mentioning names and describing stuff, but his words passed through her mind just as quickly as he said them. That was until he announced, "I'm going away for a while."

A chill crept up her arms. "Where?"

"The division is headed to Camp Forrest in Tennessee for extra training. Nothing dangerous."

"How long will you be gone?"

"We aren't going just yet but it'll be for twelve weeks."

"Bill, it's nice and all that you're here talking about these things with me but I have to know something."

His attention went back to the photos, admiring them with pride.

"Bill."

He looked at her, surprised like he hadn't realized she was still talking. "What?"

Betty wrung her hands. "You act like you want to be serious with me."

He blinked repeatedly as if trying to make sense of what Betty just told him. "I'm sorry. I've got a lot on my mind. Things are happening in which I'm involved. Of course I'm serious about you. If I wasn't, why would I be here?"

He placed the photos on the coffee table. He reached behind Betty and stretched his arm across her shoulders. He brought his face close to hers and for Betty it was like all that was good and possible between them was about to happen.

December 7, 1941, Camp Forrest, Tennessee

The bugler's call for reveille echoed through the barracks. This being Sunday, Bill had the day off and since he wasn't on any duty roster, he could lay in his bunk and get up at his leisure. He rolled onto his side to face the pot-bellied stove in the middle of the barrack's floor and pulled the sheets and the army-issue wool blanket tight around him. As he appreciated the stove's warmth, he thought about Betty, then his mom and sisters. Where was Carl Ladwig? Bill knew that now that Carl was married, he'd put in for a deferment. Bill's musings returned to Betty and he reflected how lucky he was to have her as his girl. He promised himself that when he returned to Chicago he'd be more attentive to her. He really, really liked Betty. Was he in love? *If so, I need to let her know.*

He let the thought go. *Things work out. They always do.* However, he'd make sure Betty would know how serious he was about them being together.

Bill lay in his bunk until eight, proud of the fact that his extra time in the sack was considered bona fide goldbricking hours according to army standards. By nine he was eating breakfast at the battalion mess hall, having showered and shaved and dressed in his fatigues. Many of the tables were empty as those who could were taking advantage of a weekend pass to nearby Tullahoma. Bill had been there. Problem was, there was less to do in that little sparrow fart of a town than there was at the camp, other than to get into trouble with the locals.

He returned to his barracks where he thumbed through dog-eared magazines. He didn't mind having nothing to do. During the week, the army kept him plenty busy.

When the canteen opened at noon, he moseyed over there and bought gum and toothpaste. Several other sad sacks from the company invited him to a pick-up game of baseball.

They assembled at the athletic field and organized themselves into teams. Someone passed out gloves and baseballs. Bill trotted to right field and played catch with the center fielder. The opposing team picked up bats to practice their swings and traded insults with Bill's side.

The winter sun shone bright upon them. All of life's problems would have to wait until tomorrow.

A bugle sounded through the camp's public address system. The brassy, melancholy melody echoed across the camp. Everyone on the baseball field faced the pole behind the backstop where the closest loudspeaker hung and listened, perplexed at this unexpected interruption in the day's relaxed routine.

A series of clicks emanated from the loudspeaker, then a man in gravelly voice spoke: "Attention in the camp. Early this morning, the Japanese attacked Pearl Harbor. All furloughs and passes are canceled. Those not on duty are to report to their company orderly rooms and await further instructions." The man quit talking and the soldiers stared at the loudspeaker, expecting more news.

The guy playing shortstop wrinkled his face, squinting, and exclaimed, "The Japs? I thought we were worried about the Germans. Anyway, where is Pearl Harbor?"

"Beats me," the pitcher remarked. "Seems President Roosevelt finally got the war he's been itching for."

When they realized that no more information was forthcoming over the loudspeaker, everyone congregated on home plate and solemnly dumped their gloves, the balls, and bats in a pile.

Bill regarded the rows of barracks arranged in army-straight lines and perfect right angles. In the distance, he heard a sergeant bark orders as if about to march his troops into immediate combat.

The world seemed to fold on itself and in the middle of the creases sat Bill. He panned the other soldier's faces. Some remained staring at the loudspeaker. Others shuffled in place and kicked the dirt. They were all separate yet together as history swept them together in one direction. Toward war.

4

January 7, 1942

A snowy afternoon cast its frigid pall over Chicago. The bitter temperatures reminded everyone of the bad news that continued into the new year. Things weren't going well. The war in Europe raged like a bonfire while the Japanese continued to rampage unchecked in the Pacific.

Down on the street, Betty and Bill proceeded arm-in-arm, heads down, grimacing against the icy slap of freezing air. He wore his army-issue overcoat with the collar flipped up and his head scrunched between the big flaps of wool to protect his ears. Snow dusted his service cap. Betty was swaddled in a tweedy wool coat with a fur collar. A scarf tied around her head kept her ears warm and the wind from taking her hat. It was a miserable time to be outside but both Bill and Betty wanted to be alone and away from relatives and friends. After all, Bill would be leaving soon for training camp.

When they made this date, Betty had hoped for a leisurely stroll and an easy conversation. Somehow, in her eagerness to be with Bill she'd forgotten about Chicago's infamous winter storms. The prudent choice would have been to remain indoors. After all, Betty was known as the prudent one. What made her overlook the storm was that Bill was alongside her. His presence beside her made the cold weather that much more bearable.

She squeezed his arm and he squeezed back.

"Let's get out of this nasty weather," he said.

They were still several blocks from the movie theater, their destination. Betty glanced about. "And go where?"

He made an abrupt turn, pulling her along. They darted into a hotel.

Betty's breath hitched. *A hotel? What was Bill thinking?*

He held the door open for her to enter, which she did, hesitantly. She looked about the lobby and regarded the surroundings. Shabby furniture, carpet worn in strips and pockmarked with cigarette burns. Air that smelled of ash trays. The hotel was the sort used by traveling businessmen on a tight budget, and Betty was a little put off by Bill bringing her here.

"We're not getting a room, are we?" she whispered, anxious. Respectable single women did not visit such hotels.

Bill wrinkled his brow. "What? Of course not. Like I said, we had to get out of that storm." He mimicked shaking from cold and said, *"Brrr."* He steered her toward a sofa and an armchair arranged close to a radiator.

At the far end of the lobby, a balding clerk with a thin mustache was busy behind the counter, sweeping the floor with a broom, smoke curling from a cigar parked nearby. He looked up.

Bill waved. "We're waiting for a couple of friends. They'll be along shortly."

The clerk scowled. "They got a room?"

"Sure they do. Otherwise, why tell us to meet them here?" Bill then added, muttering softly, "This dump." He brushed snow from Betty's shoulders.

The clerk shrugged and resumed his chores.

As she removed her gloves and scarf she remarked to herself how easy Bill seem to skate through life. Walking in here and claiming a space was so typically Bill, acting like he was doing this hotel a favor just by his presence. The way he confidently helped himself to his environment comforted her. Betty was the careful one, the planner, the one who kept a monthly calendar and a daily schedule. She made lists. She set goals.

Bill did none of these things. He simply went out and improvised as the day went along, a skill that amazed her. In this case, he got them in here with a white lie, something she would never do. Truth was, she admired him for it. Since war was declared, Betty had the sense of being swept away by events, completely out of control. Bill showed no such concerns.

When he reached for her coat and hat, Bill paused. "What's that look?"

"What look?"

"That one. The one you're giving me." For someone remarkably self-centered, Bill could be quite perceptive.

Betty wanted to share her worries but knew that Bill didn't like to dwell on the negative. He was like a sailboat that managed to tack and make gains even against a headwind.

She warmed her hands on the radiator. "I'm glad we stopped in here."

Slush puddled on the threadbare carpet around their shoes. Bill hung her coat and hat on an adjacent coat rack, then removed his service cap, unbuttoned his overcoat, shook off the snow, and hung them both on the rack next to Betty's. He unwound his army-issue scarf from around his neck and hung that too.

Betty noticed that he moved with care and a bit of ceremony. She remained standing until he gestured gallantly that she take a seat on the sofa. Sitting at one end, she expected him to sit next to her. Instead, he took the armchair. He checked his watch. "We won't make the five o'clock movie. I guess that leaves dinner."

"Dinner is fine."

Bill drummed his fingers on the chair's armrests.

"Something on your mind?" she asked.

He held his fingers still. He smiled at her. "Just you. Is that a crime?"

Betty felt the weight of current events pressing upon her. She remembered her history lessons and it was all stories about someone else. She never gave a thought to the women left behind when their men marched off to war. And she never thought much about the war widows. Now there were going to be a lot of war widows.

Bill reached and patted her hand. "You're looking a bit glum. Like you're the one on the way to some Camp Swampy in the South."

"Sorry." She kept her next thoughts to herself. *It's that now I have someone to lose.*

Betty had heard that opposites attract and for her and Bill this was true. Betty liked order and predictability. But with the onset of war, there was chaos and a loss of control. It seemed pointless to make plans since anything might happen.

Bill's optimism warmed her better than the radiator next to them. Outwardly, for her, things hadn't gotten worse. In fact, things had even improved. The economy was speeding up. There were new jobs with better wages.

The big worry was what was going to happen to Bill? She allowed in an easy tone, "Gossip is that the 33rd Division will remain stateside in case of an invasion."

Bill's eyes crinkled a bit to acknowledge that he had heard her but made no comment. Then he grinned. "I wouldn't worry a bit about the 33rd Division."

A week later, Betty would realize that Bill had slyly admitted that he no longer belonged to the National Guard or to the 33rd Division.

Bill slid into the coffee shop booth. Carl Ladwig sat on the opposite side, nursing a cup of coffee.

"How's married life?" Bill said. He hailed a waitress who brought a cup, filled it from a carafe and refreshed Carl's java.

Carl stirred in cream and sugar. "Pretty good. I mean, if it wasn't for the war, I'd have nothing to complain about."

He glanced at Bill's uniform. "So they said, on account of new army directives, I probably wouldn't be sent to Europe. When I do go in, I'll most likely be fighting the Japs."

Bill sipped from his cup. His time in the army had taught him to appreciate black coffee. "That doesn't make sense. Wouldn't the military want someone who knows the German language and culture?"

"I told that to the recruiter."

"What did he say?"

"He said, 'You better learn quick that the military way and making sense don't always agree.

And when you wear olive drab, you better do things the military way.' "

Bill smirked. "Ain't that the truth"

"And you? You told me you had news."

"Yeah. This." Bill unfolded a document on the table. "Here's my copy of my enlistment contract."

"I thought you were already in?"

"In the case of a national emergency, the law lets me opt out of the guard if I choose active duty. So I signed up for the Army Air Force."

Carl's eyebrows lifted. "As a pilot?"

Bill waved his hands. "Not that."

"Then what? Why?"

"For Betty," Bill replied. "If I volunteer for an aircrew position, on account of my prior service, I get an immediate promotion to corporal and then to sergeant on completion of training. Plus, as long as I'm flying, I get half my base pay extra. She's going to need the money. I leave in two weeks."

"You're doing this for Betty?" Carl narrowed his eyes. "What do you have in mind?"

"When I told everyone that I'd met the woman I was going to marry, I wasn't kidding."

January 16, 1942

Bill surveyed the landscape as the bus rolled past the wooden sign welcoming them to *Kessler Field, Mississippi. Army Air*

Force. There wasn't much. A lot of palm trees and brush. The bus crunched over gravel along a recently scraped road through the grass and weeds. He shared a bench seat with Harold Emerson. They hadn't met until this bus ride, and during conversation in the long hours cooped together, Bill learned that Harold was from west of Chicago—Elmhurst as a matter of fact—and like Bill, he was also a former guardsman who had joined the Army Air Force.

The bus lurched to a halt. Since Harold had the window seat, Bill leaned past him to see what else waited for them. The bus had pulled short outside a recently constructed two-story wooden building marked *Headquarters* that looked like every other building marked *Headquarters* they'd seen on this trip. In front of the building, the American flag hung from a pole surrounded by a circle of rocks painted white.

The bus door clattered open. Everyone scrambled to retrieve their bags. Outside, a sergeant in khakis barked for everyone to climb out and quit their lollygagging. Laden with duffel bags, the soldiers shuffled toward the front of the bus, pivoted for the door, then stepped outside into the cool, humid air.

Bill fell into formation with the others. He was already an old hand with the army "hurry up and wait."

An airplane droned overhead. Bill shaded his eyes to study it. The airplane was a twin-engine type that he didn't recognize. Sunlight gleamed from its fuselage as if beckoning him and assuring that he had made the right choice in becoming a member of the Army Air Force.

At the sound of a truck's horn, the sergeant ordered everyone to step back from the road. A convoy of civilian trucks laden with construction material rumbled past. Bill traded gazes with the Black men in patched, work clothes riding on the piles of lumber in the truck beds.

The sergeant took roll call and marched the soldiers down the street past a row of recently constructed wooden buildings. Behind them spread an array of big olive-green army tents. Bill, Harold, and ten others were assigned to one tent. Their home for now.

Another sergeant waited in the tent. He read "O'Loughlin," from a clipboard and pointed to a cot and an open footlocker. Harold was assigned the next cot over. Bill noted the primitive conditions but at least they had a wooden floor and a potbellied stove.

After dropping their duffel bag on their cots, the men filed into another tent where they were issued bedding and more equipment. Within an hour, Bill and his tentmates had changed into fatigue uniforms and were spending the rest of the day unloading construction materials from the trucks.

"It's pretty amazing," Harold said. He and Bill carried a sheet of plywood.

"What do you mean?" Bill replied.

"I mean," Harold said, "is how well organized the army can be. I mean, we traveled over a thousand miles by bus and there's a cot with my name waiting for me. Now all these barracks arrive in kits, everything precut, with all the nails and everything. All we got to do is put them together. On top of that, we get three square meals a day and a paycheck."

Bill said, "You didn't grow up with much, did you?"

"Naw," Harold replied, "my folks were on relief most of the time."

"I can tell," Bill said.

They dropped the sheet onto a stack of plywood. *Whap!*

Harold fished a packet of Lucky Strikes from his shirt pocket. He offered one to Bill, who took it with a friendly smile.

"Take a look at that." Harold pointed to the bustle around them. Teams of Black men dug trenches for foundations, extending the reach of the camp's layout. Other men relayed wheelbarrows of cement mix, which they dumped into the readied foundations. Beyond them, still more soldiers in army fatigues hammered together wooden studs, creating the frames for barracks, which would be covered in plywood, then asbestos cladding, and finally clapboard siding. Army engineers would apply the finishing touches of roofing, plumbing, and electrical wiring. With so much work going on at once, it was like being inside a beehive.

Harold puffed on his cigarette. "Pretty amazing?"

Bill had to agree that it was.

"You know what would be really amazing?" a sergeant growled from behind them, startling both men. "Would be for you two goldbricks to get back to work."

Three days later, Bill and the others from his tent were assigned to a newly constructed barracks that smelled of wet paint. From then on, life in Kessler Field settled into a familiar military routine. The reveille bugled at 6 a.m. The barracks' lights blared on, signaling that though the sun wouldn't rise for another fifty minutes, the training day had begun. Bill joined the mad scramble to the latrine where men crowded around sinks and mirrors to shave. First formation roll call. Then marching in battalion mass to the athletic field where a muscular sergeant on a platform led them for an hour of calisthenics and drills. Then back to the barracks to clean up, followed by breakfast, and standing at 8 a.m. formation for the day's training.

"Corporal O'Loughlin." The instructor's voice buzzed through the earphones in Bill's cloth flight helmet.

He was in the high-altitude chamber, sitting on a bench with his fellow students. He breathed through the rubber mask attached to his helmet. The air pressure in the chamber had been reduced to mimic that at high-altitude. As each man exhaled and inhaled, the rubber bladder of his air hose expanded and contracted. The air hose connected to the oxygen regulator along the bench by each man's right knee. A cat's eye indicator on the regulator winked in rhythm to the man's breathing, showing white when he inhaled, black when he exhaled. The men were being tested as to how well they could operate the required equipment and how they would cope with oxygen starvation in the event of a malfunctioning mask. For his part, Bill enjoyed this training. It was technically exotic and, considering his expected role as an aircrewman, imminently practical.

The instructor sergeant sat behind a master console with rows of valves and gauges that controlled the individual masks. Like everyone else, he wore a helmet and mask with an intercom connection. He held up a playing card. The four of clubs. "O'Loughlin, what do you see?"

"The four of clubs," Bill answered.

The instructor plucked the next card from the stack—the king of hearts—and directed his question to Harold, who sat on the bench beside Bill.

Harold squinted at the card. If he couldn't readily identify the card, this meant trouble. His hose bladder was expanding and contracting so he was breathing. Bill checked Harold's oxygen regulator. The indicator was stuck on black, meaning he wasn't getting oxygen.

Bill grabbed Harold's hand and put it on the regulator knob, hoping to get him to react. With the onset of oxygen starvation, a man's senses got dulled quickly. They'd been taught that the effects were subtle but could become catastrophic when in flight.

The sergeant demanded, "O'Loughlin, what are you doing?"

Bill didn't know if what he was doing was wrong but it seemed to him that Harold's regulator was malfunctioning. "Emerson's equipment isn't working."

The sergeant stared at Bill. He turned a valve on his console. Harold's indicator began winking again. "Good job, O'Loughlin. I turned off Emerson's supply to demonstrate that oxygen starvation can happen without warning." The sergeant thumped the top of his console. "Everybody, listen up. Flying as aircrew is a team effort. One of your buddies is in trouble, you help him out."

Once a week, Bill was taken aloft in a Cessna AT-17 Bobcat, a small twin-engine trainer. His task was to check the airplane for airworthiness and then sit in the passenger compartment and practice operating the radio. Mostly though, the flights were to help new pilots transition from single-engine airplanes to multi-engine types. While they buzzed about, Bill looked down at the world through a side window. They cruised over the Gulf of Mexico and followed the Biloxi River as it meandered north through swamps and pine forests.

He thought about a lot of things. Like everyone else in uniform, the first question was where the war would take him? When he had signed up for the Illinois National Guard he never imagined that would start him on a path that led him to this seat on an airplane orbiting the Mississippi landscape.

But his favorite musings were of Betty and how lucky he was to have met her. She'd been a trooper when he told her about joining the Army Air Force.

"You know best," was what she had said, her voice both hopeful and sad.

Committing himself to their relationship added a direction and a purpose that strengthened Bill. How much stronger would that direction and purpose be when he deepened his commitment to Betty?

5

❖

January 28, 1942

Dear Eileen,

Hey sis, how are you? How's the gang? I hope I don't ruin my reputation as the man of the house if I mention how much I miss you and Mom and everybody else.

I'm still at Kessler Field, outside Biloxi, which rates as a big city in these parts. I guess in better times, Biloxi has its charms, being located right along the coast. Summers I'm told, the beaches are nice and people come from all over. But now the city has the feel of a run-down wharf with everything you think that means. Plenty of opportunities to get into trouble. It's the South and so the locals pretend they're too pious to drink but the place is lousy with honky tonks and illegal saloons and rough characters. Each Monday morning plenty of our boys wind up on the police blotter and spend time in the stockade.

Last week my squadron received our aircraft assignments. For us enlisted men, it means either combat or transport, the difference being planes with guns or without them. Since there is a shooting war going on, in case you haven't noticed, most of the assignments are for combat types, yours truly included. We started what they call "Flexible Gunnery Training." Mostly we learned how to operate machine guns like what we'll have on the airplanes. To pass the first block of training we had to troubleshoot the guns and then take them apart/put back together while blindfolded and wearing gloves. Being from Chicago I was plenty used to wearing winter gloves so this part of the training was a piece o' cake.

Yesterday we did live-fire drills which are kinda fun. We take turns shooting a machine gun at a plywood square mounted on top of a truck as it scoots back-and-forth across the firing range. The range is at the beach and we got a late start in the shooting on account of a fishing boat being inside the off-limits area where the bullets hit the water. The area is marked by buoys so the guy knew what he was doing. The local fishermen get money from the army for their troubles but they are a crusty stubborn lot who don't like the government telling them what they can or can't do. A boat from Range Control had to go out there and convince the fisherman that he was holding up the war effort. What a lug.

Overall, everything around here seems slapped together. Some of the instructors have less time in uniform than I do, even the officers. We use a lot of pretend "mock ups" since we don't have the actual devices handy to train on. They keep telling us that when we get to our operational squadrons we'll get our hands on the for-real equipment. I hope so. On the plus side, we get plenty to eat but because of all the physical training, I won't get fat, don't you worry.

Give my regards to everybody. Give Mom a big hug and tell her I miss her cooking. I'll let you know when I can make my way back to Chicago.

Love,

Bill aka Corporal William M. O'Loughlin, USAAF

In early February, Bill and his fellow students were trucked to the airfield hangers for the next phase of Flexible Gunnery Training. Recently, working aircraft turrets from Bendix, General Electric, and Emerson had arrived for use by the mechanics and the aircrews.

The turrets were domes made of curved transparent acrylic with metal framing that sat atop a short aluminum sleeve about three feet in diameter. The sleeve was, in turn, mounted in a support frame connected to electrical or hydraulic power. The men would take turns climbing inside from the bottom and getting comfortable on the seat with the receiver of a .50 caliber Browning machine gun just inches from either ear. A metal control box with electrical switches sat at chest level. Their hands rested naturally on a pair of handles that operated the turret and the guns, which they aimed through a round optical sight.

When the turret powered up, the mechanisms hummed as if the contraption was alive. Manipulating the control handles, the turret rotated easily and the guns likewise elevated and depressed. To Bill, the turrets were futuristic, mechanical wonders.

But the reality was that these turrets were a necessary defense against attacks by the feared German Messerschmitt and Japanese Zero fighters. Still, Bill mused, a couple of .50 caliber machine guns like these shoved up your nostrils would make any enemy pilot question his determination.

February 10, 1942
Bill and two other students were hunkered inside an AT-18 Hudson trainer, watching their breath plume in the cold air as they waited their turn for live-fire turret training. Because it was still winter and they were up at altitude, they wore fleece-lined leather helmets and insulated leather coveralls over their regular duty uniforms. The overalls kept Bill warm enough but since he hadn't been issued insulated boots, he shuffled his regular boots back and forth across the floor to keep his feet from freezing.

The instructor waved him aft toward the turret. It was identical to the one they had been training in so with little effort he ducked under the frame and wormed his way into the seat. When he poked his head into the transparent dome, he reacted by squinting at the sudden glare of sunlight— so bright that it hurt. He palmed his goggles to slide them down over his eyes and flip the tinted lenses into place. Once situated, he plugged into the intercom. Upon hearing the headset buzz he pressed the *Talk* button on the control handset. "I'm ready."

"Go ahead," the instructor replied through the intercom. Bill activated the power switches. He rotated the turret, amazed by the aerial panorama as he traversed in a circle, first to the left, then the right. Sunlight glinted off the airplane's aluminum fuselage, engine nacelles, and wings. Far below, a gentle fog muted the Mississippi landscape.

He positioned the turret so it faced aft. In the distance, an airplane gained on them, its propeller disk shining like a silver coin.

The pilot announced over the intercom, "Target tug coming around to starboard."

"Got it," Bill said.

The tug was a Douglas A-33, a single-engine monoplane. Bill kept the turret aimed to the rear since to track the tug with loaded machine guns was a disciplinary offense. These live-fire exercises were dangerous enough. The target, a red and white cloth banner about twenty feet long, fluttered behind the A-33. As the tug continued forward, a cable connected to the target began to unspool from a winch inside the airplane's fuselage. Farther and farther the target lagged behind the tug until it sailed a half mile away. Then the A-33 accelerated, passed the AT-18, and brought the target closer.

"She's coming into position," the pilot said. "Fire when ready."

"Roger. Switches to fire." Bill flicked the switches on the control box. The gun's ARMED lights flashed red. The AT-18 was flying at a steady 175 knots with the tug overtaking them at 225 knots and at a slightly higher altitude. The target passed within three hundred yards. By comparison, firing at a ground target was easy enough as you could see where the bullets struck the earth and adjust aim from that. But shooting at an aerial target proved a challenge, even for a softball pitch like this one since you didn't know precisely where the bullets were going. They were trained in a technique called "position aiming," which was how to compensate for an enemy's attack along what was known as the "pursuit slope."

Bill set the reticle on the target, compensated for lead and angle of the slope, then squeezed the control handle triggers. The machine guns hammered loud, and balls of flame burst from the muzzles. The turret shuddered from the percussive blasts.

Like he'd been taught, Bill fired a short burst, then released the triggers. The guns fell silent. Gun smoke and the odor of hot oil swirled inside the turret.

Bill studied the target and couldn't see if he'd hit it or not. He renewed his focus through the gun sight and fired another burst. Glancing at the round counter, he'd fired forty-two cartridges so far. He managed two more bursts until the target had advanced beyond the designated oblique angle to the AT-18.

"Cease fire," the pilot said. With all the precautionary measures in place, this live-fire practice seemed safe enough until you considered that you had a student firing a pair of heavy machine guns in your direction.

The AT-18 banked slightly to the right and approached the target. Anxious to see how well he'd done, Bill raised in his seat until the top of his head bumped the turret canopy. A series of holes dotted the target. If the enemy wasn't destroyed, he was sure hurting.

"Good job," the pilot said, affirming Bill's sense of accomplishment. "Who was shooting?"

Bill instantly keyed the intercom. "O'Loughlin."

"You're a natural at this."

"Of course," Bill replied. "I am from Chicago."

February 24, 1942

Princess,

Sorry I haven't answered your letters. We finally got our crew position assignments and our orders to an operation unit, and because of that there's a lot of shuffling around from place to place. In the great wisdom of the Army Air Force I've been assigned as a flight engineer on a B-25 Mitchell bomber.

Kinda ironic, no? My dad was a building engineer and it was something I didn't want to do and yet here I am . . . a flight engineer. Must be in the blood. Basically, I stay after the mechanics and ground crew to make sure things on my airplane are up to snuff. And when we're in the air I help the pilots monitor the engines and other mechanical and electrical gizmos. My other duties are as a gunner.

For flight engineer training I'm being sent to California to the factory where they make the B-25s. Though this adds more time to us being apart, the good news is that when I'm done I get a week's furlough before I report to Columbia. So it seems that a visit by a special guy is in your cards.

How is everybody? My sister Eileen writes that you visit my mom on occasion. That's great. I know she worries about me for some reason. But I'm doing okay though in the army the O'Loughlin charm doesn't work quite as well as it does in Chicago. Miss you.

Love,

Bill

March 10, 1942

The Trailways bus pulled to a halt outside the Army Air Force processing center at Mines Airfield, Inglewood, California. When Bill filed out of the bus he noticed the air had a welcoming ocean crispness to it like in Mississippi, but without the threat of an oppressive Gulf Coast humidity.

Other than Hollywood, Los Angeles, and the beach, Bill didn't know much about Southern California. From this present perspective, lined up with his fellow students, Mines Airfield appeared exceptionally flat, with a gray haze obscuring hills to the north. Aircraft droned overhead and more aircraft were parked on a tarmac that stretched for a mile in three directions.

Mines Airfield was a curious mix of military and civilians. It was adjacent to the massive North American Aviation manufacturing plant. Since he was to be a flight engineer on a B-25 he wasn't surprised to see rows and rows of the twin-engine bombers.

Bill learned these particular airplanes were the new and more advanced B-25Cs. An almost identical version, the B-25D, was being produced at the Kansas City plant.

He was grouped with ten classmates for the flight engineer curriculum. While the cadre were all from the army, most of his instructors were civilians, and most of them techs coming directly from the assembly line. No one was more familiar with the B-25 than they were. Unlike at Kessler Field where they often had to make do with mock ups, here they got to train on the actual examples that progressed along the assembly line.

His days began in typical military fashion with 6 a.m. wakeup but no reveille bugle as an orderly went through the barracks and banged on doors instead. Then first formation, physical training, breakfast, and by nine, they were queued to enter the airfield through one of the security gates. Although Bill was in military uniform, he couldn't go through the gate without someone from his training outfit verifying who he was and checking his name off the day's roster. Then he was issued the day's security badge, a metal button about an inch-and-half in diameter, and color-coded by day—orange, yellow, white, blue, green—and printed with the appropriate department number. Bill pinned the button above the left front pocket of his uniform and picked up his training workbook, stamped *Confidential.* Woe to anyone who lost their copy.

Compared to his previous military experience, the training atmosphere was surprisingly relaxed. You were treated like a bona fide adult. You were told to be somewhere and you showed up on time. You paid close attention as you were expected to be a quick study. The big motivator was that to wash out of the program put you in the hopper for the infantry.

In his first days, Bill toured the entire manufacturing process, from the receiving rooms for the parts, to the foundries and machining rooms, to the assembly lines where the airplane took shape. The North American plant was over-whelming, large enough to cover several football fields under one continuous roof. On top of that, the facility churned with constant activity, 24 hours a day.

Bill became a walking encyclopedia on the B-25C, an improved version of the type used in the Doolittle raid. Wing span of 57 feet, 7 inches. Length of 54 feet, 1 inch. Empty weight of 19,800 pounds and a gross takeoff weight of 35,000 pounds.

Powered by a pair of Wright Double Cyclone R-2600-13 14-cylinder, air-cooled radial engines, each capable of gen-erating 1,700 horsepower. Maximum airspeed of 284 mph and cruise at 233 mph with a bomb load of 3,000 pounds. Internal fuel capacity of 640 gallons allowed for a range of 1,500 miles, which could be extended by adding external and internal tanks that brought the total fuel capacity to 1,255 gallons.

The bombers left the plant with two powered turrets, each sporting a pair of .50 caliber machine guns. The up-per turret was mounted mid-ship behind the bomb bay and operated by a gunner sitting in a Plexiglas dome with metal bracing. The lower turret fit flush into the belly and would be extended to defend against enemy fighters. However, this turret was remotely operated and aimed through a complex arrangement of sighting mirrors.

A B-25 would take shape as a basic skeleton at one end of the long assembly line and advanced steadily, teams of workers adding components. By the next day, the bomber and its engines, minus the outer wing panels, guns, and radios would be wheeled to the final "outdoor" assembly area. One bomber per hour, every hour. All the while, inspectors crawled under, over, around, and inside the airplanes. The process was a technical miracle. Tens of thousands of pieces had to made and fitted together with the precision of a watch.

What put all this industrial effort into perspective was when one of his sergeant instructors told him that the reason they had to make so many airplanes was to put more bombers in the air than the enemy could shoot down.

March 22, 1942

Sweetheart,

How are you? It's Sunday, our only full day off. Most of the other fellas have taken a pass for Los Angeles. Trollies run all day, so there's no problem getting from place to place. But since I'm saving my pennies for a certain someone, I'll make my way to Marina Del Rey and spend the day there. Maybe do some fishing or just sight-seeing.

It's a different world here. The plant is enormous. So much going on. Plus we get everything we need. The food is plentiful and tasty. I think when the army finds out how good we have it here, that they'll shut this place down. Ha!

What's really amazing are all the women working in the plant. They work the foundries, the lathes, the rivet guns, everything. About half of them are from around here, the rest from all over. The pay is pretty good, too. You might want to think about coming out here and applying. Don't worry about qualifications. They train you for the skills they need. Someone as sharp as you wouldn't have a problem getting a great job. Just an idea.

How are Florence, Eileen, and Pat? Have you been by to see my sister Marce and her lively gang?

Maybe you can manage a trip out here. I'd give you the premium O'Loughin tour. The area is very pretty. Orange trees everywhere. The beaches are nice. Too bad there's war on. But it won't last forever. I sure do miss you.

Love,

Bill

6

June 12, 1942

Bill had been to Chicago's Union Station plenty of times, but he didn't remember the place being as crowded as it was this afternoon. When he had made arrangements with Betty to meet at the station, he hadn't considered such a crowd and more to the point, that he would be one of hundreds of men in uniform swarming across the platform. In his left hand he carried his AWOL bag and his duffel bag was slung over his right shoulder. He shoehorned his way through the teeming, noisy mob toward the Great Hall.

Even before the war, when thousands mingled through the cavernous space beneath its tall and impressive skylight, the Great Hall was a challenging place to meet people. Now it was bedlam.

Bill lifted on tiptoes to get a better view, but all he saw were heads bobbing in every direction. Disembodied hands waved. When he heard a woman shout, "Bill!" his pulse jumped, then flattened when the voice was smothered in the din.

After he pushed for several minutes through the jostling masses of Marines, sailors, and fellow soldiers, the crowd finally thinned out. He swung the duffel bag off his back and dropped it beside a bench.

Then he heard his name again. "Bill!" His ears searched through the cacophony in the vain hope that he hadn't been hearing things.

"Over here!"

He pivoted in place, frustration rising in him as he kept losing the voice in the rumble.

A delicate hand waved. Then he saw Betty's bounce of blond hair. She scooted past a family clustered around a sailor. Waving fingers, Betty finally rushed into view. She wore a yellow dress with white trim and a matching hat. Bill's sister, Eileen, was with her, wearing a beige dress printed with blue flowers.

The closer Betty scrambled toward him, the more he focused on her big eyes and her broad smile. She crushed into him, hugging with all her might.

He hugged her back, becoming again acquainted with her warmth, her youthful firmness, and the delicious smell of her golden hair.

They kissed, hugged once more, then separated just enough to hold one another at arms' length. "Look at you," she said breathlessly, her eyes ranging over him. "A sergeant?"

He replied with a self-deprecating smile. "Who would've known?"

Eileen stepped behind Betty, grinning uncomfortably as if aware that she was a third wheel at this homecoming. Bill let go of Betty's hand and reached for Eileen. She leaned into him for a quick hug, then slapped his shoulder. "You look good. Put on some weight."

He flexed his upper body. "More like muscle. If there's one thing the army believes in, it's physical training."

Betty took the AWOL bag from his hand. "Come on, let's find some place to eat. A couple of Chicago steaks, yes?"

Bill hefted the duffel bag over a shoulder. As he walked, he felt the envy of the GIs at the station who saw him stroll past with a beautiful young woman on either arm.

Bill finished his second helping of blueberry pie. It was a surreal experience, holding court in his mother's kitchen, surrounded by women, he being the only man on the premises. Back at Kessler Field, he would go days before seeing a woman, let alone actually talk to one. Mines Airfield was different as the work force at the North American plant was fifty percent female.

As he regaled his family with anecdotes about his training as an aircrewman, they hung on every word.

"Do they let you fly the plane?" his sister Pat asked.

"Actually, they do. As flight engineer one of my duties is co-pilot when needed." He spared his family the instructional-manual explanation as to why he would need to serve as co-pilot, should either the pilot or the co-pilot become *incapacitated.*

Betty sat beside him, her hand clasping his beneath the table. She was a beacon of hope and possibilities, and her admiration of Bill shone through her lovely, expressive eyes.

He'd drawn a diagram of the B-25 on a sheet of paper to illustrate what he was responsible for. The fuel system. The hydraulic system. The electrical system. He checked anything fitted into the bomb bay: the auxiliary fuel tanks, bombs of course, and depending on the mission, a Mark 13 aerial torpedo.

"Is it dangerous?" his mother asked.

The answer was, *Yes.* Flying was so dangerous that he got flight pay, which was the reason he had signed up for the Army Air Force and as an aircrewman.

"I wouldn't worry about it, Mother," he replied in an aw-shucks tone. "They train us well and we have the best equipment in the world."

Her eyes remained heavy with concern.

To change the subject he said, "What's really keen is flying over the coastline. Look to one side and it's the Pacific

Ocean as far as you can see. Then to the other, California, orange groves, green hills, farm land. The ground is so varied. One minute you're flying over desert, then the next, over mountains and snow."

"This time of year?" Pat asked.

Bill nodded. Truth was, the last time he had seen snow was back in late April when they flew over Big Bear Lake but why let that spoil a good story? They wanted to hear that he'd seen snow in early summer and so he had. Plus, he had plenty of tall tales he'd picked up during idle chatter in the barracks.

He pushed his coffee cup across the table. "If I can get a refill, I'll tell you about the time I had to wrestle an alligator in the swamps of Mississippi."

Bill and Betty walked arm-in-arm down State Street, the vista lit up by neon and flashing lights. "They have blackouts in Mobile," he said, pointing at the lit marquees. "Seems the enemy uses the lights to navigate."

Betty crinkled her eyes. "Mobile? Isn't that on the Gulf of Mexico? You mean the enemy has ships there?"

"U-boats . . . German submarines," he said. "Then in California, we're told to keep an eye peeled for Japanese submarines. They did shell Santa Barbara."

Betty whispered, "Wow." After a moment, she added, "I heard they're going to black out the skylight over the Great Hall in Union Station."

"Really?" Bill thought his was an extraneous measure because if the enemy ever got near enough to bomb Chicago, then the war was going very badly.

He grew silent, the dark future intruding into his thoughts. Day after tomorrow, he'd be leaving for Columbia.

Betty brushed against him. "The Bill I know is seldom this quiet."

"Just thinking," he answered. "Remember when I asked you to consider going out to California? There are lots of jobs, begging for good people."

Betty squeezed his arm. "I thought about it. But you won't be there, so what's the point?"

"The pay's great."

"I thought about that, too. But I want to stay close to my family and yours as well. Living with my mom keeps my expenses down, something else to consider."

Bill put his arm over her shoulder and drew her close. *Betty, always the planner, always thinking things through. Things between us are going to work out very well.*

June 29, 1942

Darling,

Great news! Got my promotion to staff sergeant. Got my new stripes pinned to my sleeve during the promotion ceremony. They look good. And I get a bump in pay.

Hope you are doing as well as I am. Pass my regards to Eileen, my mom, and my other sisters. I really do miss mom's cooking. Yours as well.

I'm in South Carolina, at Columbia Army Airfield just outside Columbia. This last year I've seen so much of the country courtesy of Uncle Sam. Oklahoma. Tennessee. Mississippi. California. Now South Carolina. I was here last November for training when I was in the Illinois Guard.

Though Columbia is in the South, it is a lot different than Mobile. The people here really think highly of themselves. In Mobile, the folks were always scheming up ways to take your money, in Columbia they act like they're doing us a favor by letting us stay here. Of course, not everybody is that way. In fact, some of the boys in the outfit have met sweethearts among these southern belles.

This airfield has already earned its place in the history books. This was where Colonel Doolittle trained his crews for the raid on Tokyo. Imagine flying B-25s off a carrier like they did! I don't think we'll be hitting the Japanese home islands again for a while but it was great to hear that we gave Tojo a small dose of his own bitter medicine.

Our living arrangements are fairly comfortable. We have single cots instead of bunk beds. Not much privacy though, as we're still quartered in open bays. Since I doubt I'll get another furlough anytime soon, I hope you manage to come out this way. It's really pretty here and I'm sure you'd enjoy the sights. Besides, I'd love to see you.

I miss you.

Love, Bill . . . Staff Sergeant William M. O'Loughlin, Army Air Force

August 10, 1942

Four days earlier, Bill's unit was finally activated. The ceremony was a large formation where he stood sweating under the sun while a general read a speech, some congressmen added a few words, and then the unit colors were presented for the 321st Bombardment Group and its four squadrons. Bill now belonged to the 447th Bomber Squadron. After the ceremony, Bill and the rest of his buddies marched in a pass in review.

The men in the group were assigned to bunks in alphabetical order rather than by squadron or job type. The guy in the next bed over was Joe Parisi, also from Chicago, who though quiet most of the time, didn't hesitate to share his opinions. He was posted to administrative support and so didn't fly. "Which was all right by me," he declared. "You can keep your flight pay. I'll keep my ass out of harm's way."

Joe fussed with a pencil-thin mustache. When in civilian clothes, he was a snappy dresser. Bill liked to look good as well, but with the prospect of being deployed overseas, there seemed little point in spending his pay on civilian clothes. So, he mailed as much money as he could home to his mom.

Bill looked over his stack of letters from Betty. Her birthday had been just a few days ago. Scuttlebutt was that by the middle of next year, they'd be deployed to a combat theater, which meant fighting either the Germans or the Japanese.

He had a big decision to make, one that involved Betty, and before he made that decision, he made an appointment to see the bombardment group's chaplain and ask about the process for getting married.

7

August 30, 1942

Bill combed his wavy, damp hair into place and splashed on cologne. He slipped into his shirt, newly retrieved from the laundry, and enjoyed the sensation of forcing his arms through the stiff, pasted-together-with-starch sleeves. "Breaking starch," the army called it. He had a lot on his mind and he was so giddy with anticipation that he found himself humming.

Joe Parisi lounged on his nearby cot and cupped a tin can that he used as an ashtray. "I don't know why you're here in the barracks instead of spending time with Betty."

Actually, Bill had spent most of yesterday with Betty, having greeted her at the train station, showed her the sights of Columbia, then booked her into the Jefferson Hotel downtown. He returned to the base so as to not use up his furlough.

Bill cinched his necktie. "It's bad luck for the groom to see the bride before the wedding."

"Yeah, if you wanna believe that luck stuff," Joe replied. He dug a packet of Chesterfields from his shirt pocket. He shook the packet and grimaced when he noted it was empty. "Can I bum a couple of smokes off you?"

Bill patted his trouser pockets. "I'm out too. Seems my nerves finally got to me."

"Crap," Joe said sourly and swung his feet to the floor. "I'm heading over to the canteen."

"Grab me a pack," Bill said. "As soon as I get dressed, I gotta catch a cab."

Joe tied on his athletic sneakers and shrugged into a jersey top. He headed out of the barracks.

For the wedding, Bill decided to wear his service uniform, a four-button coat decorated with his insignia, and the shirt and trousers, all in olive drab and set off with a khaki tie. Bending forward to put on his low-quarters, he realized they were scuffed because he'd forgotten to polish them. He checked his watch and realized he didn't have time to give them a proper shine.

What to do? He spied Joe's low-quarters under his cot, neatly shined and lined up with his boots. Bill knew that he and Joe wore the same size shoes, 9C. Problem solved.

Bill slipped into Joe's shoes, tied them snugly and muttered, "Well, well, don't mind if I do." After cinching his tie, he shrugged into his service coat and paused to regard himself in the full-length mirror by the latrine. He thought, *I look pretty good.*

He picked up his AWOL bag and service cap, turned on his heels, and started for the group headquarters building, where cabs were always waiting.

Bill had arranged for Betty and him to be married in City Hall. As good Catholics, they would've preferred a church wedding, but arranging one required scheduling months prior, especially in Chicago if they hoped to have relatives attend. Unfortunately, the war wouldn't wait. Should anything unfortunate happen to Bill, as his wife, Betty would get survivor's benefits so a civil wedding it was.

City Hall rose before him, an imposing white structure that occupied the corner of downtown Columbia. The cab eased to a halt. After tipping the cabbie, Bill scanned the crowded sidewalk. Dozens of people were taking advantage of the balmy autumn day, unseasonably cool and quite comfortable.

Betty waved to him as she strolled along the sidewalk. She wore a white hat, and a light blue ensemble over a white blouse with ruffles down the front. Her smile seemed as wide as the sky. Bill strode to her, his heart quickening with happiness. They glided into each other's arms for a quick kiss.

"Missed you, sweetheart," he said.

"So did I," she replied, though they'd spent time together until late yesterday evening.

He surveyed the line of men in uniform and their women companions standing against the wall, the queue leading to the entrance. With so many couples eager to get married, City Hall had done the unthinkable—stay open on Sundays. Besides doing their patriotic duty, processing so many weddings was a considerable source of revenue.

Bill and Betty took their place in line, standing arm in arm. The assembly had a festive air, complete strangers sharing in the celebration. Though the specter of war loomed above them, today was a time of happiness and making plans.

Bill spied Joe Parisi approaching from the corner. Bill tightened his arm on Betty's and whispered, "Uh, oh."

Betty whispered back, "What's wrong?"

"That's Joe Parisi, one of my army buddies. I'm wearing his shoes."

Betty glanced to his feet. "Why?"

"I'll tell you later."

Joe stepped close. He wore civilian clothes. A pencil thin mustache angled above a polite but insincere smile.

Bill didn't know what to expect. Joe was a prickly sort. But when he fixed his attention on Betty, his smile warmed several degrees.

"Well, I've heard so much about you and I'm pleased to see that Bill wasn't exaggerating."

Betty nodded. "Bill's told me a lot about you," she said though he hadn't.

"He's quite the guy." Joe made it a point to glance at Bill's shoes, but his grin indicated there were no hard feelings. He slapped Bill's arm. "I'll see you later. You two love birds have a great time."

The civil marriages were processed with assembly-line regularity. Bill and Betty waited their turn for the justice of the peace to preside over their vows, they signed the certificate, paid the fee, and were soon back on the street.

Bill wanted to drape his arm over Betty's shoulders but military decorum only allowed that he offer his arm. He didn't want to tarnish the good mood with a scolding by the Courtesy Patrol.

The next stop was a photo shop where they would sit for the wedding day portrait, Bill leaning close to Betty, both beaming warm smiles. Afterwards, they headed down Assembly Street for Gervais Street, where Bill had made reservations at the Market Restaurant. And then, the two would head to the Jefferson Hotel and start their marriage.

September 12, 1942
Bill lay inside the tail gunner's position, his eyes scanning the limitless night sky, his pulse ticking several beats above normal.

The squadron was practicing night formation flying, risky enough as it was, but made even more dangerous because they flew tactical, meaning their position lights were switched off. Each aircraft was a black hulk in black space, its presence barely indicated by the dim blue lights along the rear of the fuselage. Sometimes the bombers emerged from the gloom when they were silhouetted by silvery clouds or when moonlight glinted across the wings or the fuselage. Other times, Bill caught sight of tiny flames jetting from the exhaust stacks in the engine cowlings. Keeping track of the other aircraft was crucial in avoiding a midair collision. The problem was, if you could see an aircraft, so could the enemy.

They were also practicing forward airfield deployment and so had taken off from Columbia Airfield with the plan to land and spend the night at Walterboro Army Airfield, ninety miles to the south. In the meantime, they would, as Bill noted, buzz the North Carolina sky and convert aviation gasoline into noise.

The B-25 banked into a shallow turn to port. The two bombers trailing his own slid into position one behind the other, their propeller disks shining like pewter saucers at the instant they caught the moonlight.

"All okay back there, tail gunner?" the pilot asked.

"Roger. Everyone is in line." Bill discovered that crews were not permanently assigned to one airplane. On any mission, he could be teamed with a completely different crew on a different aircraft of the squadron. When they flew, rather than be identified by name, each crewman answered by his position: turret gunner, radioman, bombardier, etc. When Bill was in the tail, he identified himself as "tail gunner," otherwise, he was "engineer." The pilot was always referred to as "the skipper."

Bill looked down upon Lake Murray and saw the outlines of their B-25s zip across the water's glossy black surface, blotting out the pattern of reflected stars.

"Okay crew," the pilot announced, "get to your landing posts."

Bill unplugged from the intercom and shimmied backwards from the tail position. A muted red glow illuminated the interior, providing only enough light for Bill to find his parachute and buckle it over his coveralls. Grasping handholds as he proceeded forward in the aircraft, he joined the turret gunner, the radioman, and the photographer who had already strapped into their seats for the landing.

Bill peered through the access port in the bulkhead that separated their compartment from the flight deck. The crimson glow from the instrument panel outlined the pilot and co-pilot, both men tense.

The B-25 had the reputation as a loud aircraft and situated where Bill was, with an engine less than eight feet away on the wing outside, it was like being seated in a tornado. His helmet and headset did little to muffle the noise. When he connected to the intercom, it squawked with the pilot and co-pilot reciting the landing checks.

"Wing de-icers . . . Off."

"Heaters . . . Off. Automatic pilot . . . Off. Superchargers . . . Low and locked."

"Booster pumps . . . On. Mixture . . . Full rich. Props . . . 2400 rpm."

"Landing gear . . . Down."

Through the deck plates, Bill sensed the groan of the hydraulics extending the landing gear and the snap when they locked into place. The aircraft descended into a slow left turn as the squadron circled the airfield to land.

Out a side window, Bill saw runway lights, two parallel lines of small lamps demarcating the strip where they would touch down. From the wings of the lead aircraft, landing lights blinked on. The pair of lights formed a plume of white glare that slanted to the ground, illuminating a yellow oval that raced across the ground. The oval grew smaller and brighter as the bomber continued on its downward angle. Bill crossed his fingers. The group had lost two bombers and their crews, both during night operations.

His bomber tipped dramatically and the airfield disappeared from view. Then they straightened and dropped. Bill tightened his hold on the seat harness.

The B-25 bounced hard. Bill jerked against his harness.

The nose dipped as the brakes were applied. The airplane lurched and continued forward.

Bill and the others in the compartment exhaled in relief. Another safe landing.

Now he could let his thoughts roam toward other concerns. His wife Betty and their future plans.

October 23, 1942

Bill stepped off the train in Chicago's Union Station. He was one in a sea of olive drab uniforms, those of the Army, the Army Air Force, and the Marines blending together. What stood out were the sailors in their white Dixie cup caps and dark blue jumpers.

In one hand, he carried his AWOL bag and in the other, a garment bag for his civilian clothes. He traveled in uniform because it let everyone know that he was no 4F malingerer, plus he received priority seating on the train and free donuts.

Making his way out of the crush of passengers to the line of cabs, he kept a lookout for Betty. She guarded a Checker cab and was easy to spot as if her smile was a magnet that drew his gaze.

He'd kept this visit on the down low because his family would feel slighted if he was in town and didn't make time for them. But he wanted to spend all of his free time with

Betty because he didn't know when he'd ship out. The pace of training had accelerated, meaning something was in. And when he did ship out, God knew when he'd return.

Betty lunged at him and kissed his cheek. "Come on," she invited breathlessly and jerked open the taxi door. The cabbie took Bill's two bags and stowed them in the trunk.

Betty climbed into the back seat and Bill slid close to her. She grabbed his hand and said to the driver, "The Sherman Hotel."

The next day, Bill put on his civilian suit, gray tweed with a double-breasted jacket. Betty slipped into a pale-yellow dress with white trim. As much as they wanted to keep this visit a secret, Betty let slip to Florence, and Bill couldn't pop into town without seeing his best friend, Carl Ladwig. They met and posed for photos, ignoring the war's distant storm clouds.

That evening, after dinner and returning in the hotel, Bill and Betty lay in bed. She rested her head on his chest. He felt the urge for a cigarette but at the moment preferred to enjoy Betty's soft breathing.

He said, "You seem preoccupied."

She asked, "Have you decided on names?"

Bill rustled. "Names for what?"

"Our children."

"You want me to come up with names without asking you?"

"I've made a list," she replied.

"I'd be surprised if you didn't," he said. "You're the most organized person I know."

"Being organized helps things work out."

Bill stayed quiet.

"Well," she said, "what's on your mind?"

"When are you going to show me the list?"

She snuggled up to him. "Later. First, we need to have a baby on the way."

The train chugged away from Union Station. Like the hundreds of GIs onboard, Bill was leaning out the window for one last glimpse of their sweethearts. Betty became lost in the mass of faces and bodies that packed the platform.

After resigning himself to the inevitable, he pulled back into the car. The other GIs who had crowded beside him likewise retreated to their seats and settled in for the long ride. Within minutes, a layer of gray cigarette smoke twisted through the railcar. A group of marines cracked open a flask of whiskey and passed it around.

Bill helped himself to a sip before handing it to the next guy.

His head swirled with conflicting thoughts. He had just left the love of his life. Betty had been teary eyed but had not cried. She was strong that way. He tried to linger on her expression, her bright eyes brimming with optimism as if she saw a future with more clarity than he did.

But there was no denying the uncertain challenges that lay ahead. He had never thought much about his place in the world. At the moment, he felt quite small, squeezed by the tectonic plates of history.

Bill inhaled deeply on his cigarette and took comfort in the warm tobacco smoke circulating through his lungs. Little pleasures like this kept him going.

He'd be back.

8

February 16, 1943

Bill learned of the 321st Bombardment Group's impending deployment through rumor. At the next formation, the first sergeant made it official. "Everyone is confined to the barracks and duty areas. No phone calls over an outside line and no outgoing mail until further notice."

The first sergeant read off a list of names, including Bill's. "Sergeant O'Loughlin, you are to report to group operations right away."

After the formation was dismissed, Bill and the other flight engineers whose names were called out—Paul Baringer, Gerritt Cook, Arthur Schwartz, Matthew Czabaj—waited for a cargo truck to take them to group operations at the airfield. During the ride, Cook and Schwartz cracked jokes but Bill was quiet. For weeks now, deployment overseas was a cloud on the horizon that had remained that way, on the horizon. Now they'd be journeying toward it, distancing themselves from their families and advancing into harm's way. Training had been hazardous enough. Now they'd be undertaking the same types of dicey missions but with someone shooting at them. If all went well, Bill would be returning to his wife and child. If things didn't go well . . . Bill felt his guts knot. He tamped down the bad feelings, preferring to embrace the positive attitude that kept everyone in the squadron sane and dedicated to their tasks.

Bill and the other flight engineers filed into Group Operations, the cavernous building converted from a warehouse. Rows of folding chairs faced a stage, behind which stood a wall covered with navigational charts that spanned the southeastern seaboard of the US, the northeastern coast of South America, the Caribbean, the western coast of Africa, and the vastness of the Atlantic Ocean in between. They recognized pilots and navigators from their squadron and sat with them. More airmen arrived, filling the seats amid a loud murmur of conversation.

Someone at the back of the room boomed, "Atten-hut!"

In a rustle of clothing and shuffling of feet, everyone grew quiet and rose to their feet. A colonel marched down the center aisle and climbed onto the stage. He took a position behind a lectern. "Take seats."

More feet shuffling. Chairs squeaked.

He began, "I am Colonel Donner, Chief of Staff of the Third Air Force. It's been my pleasure and honor to shepherd you men through some tough training. Now all that is going to be put to the test. In battle." He tipped his head toward to the wall of charts. "It should be obvious that you're being deployed to the Middle Eastern Theater. There the 321st Bombardment Group will be transferred to the 57th Bombardment Wing of the 12th Air Force. You men will join combat operations to destroy the enemy in North Africa and then chase what's left across the Mediterranean."

The colonel picked up a wooden pointer from behind the lectern and gestured to the charts. "You'll be deploying in a series of hops. The first hop will be from Columbia to airfields in southern Florida and Louisiana. The second hop will be to San Juan, Puerto Rico. Then south to Atkinson Field in British Guyana, then another hop to Belém, Brazil. Then the big hop across the Atlantic to Ascension Island. The final hop will be to Accra in Ghana." He tapped a spot on the western coast of Africa.

Bill stared at the routes, trying to comprehend the enormity of what was ahead. Before he joined the Illinois Guard, he hadn't spent but a day or two out of the state. Now he was about to fly over continents and the Atlantic Ocean like he was some kind of explorer with the *National Geographic*. His insides tugged at him, toward Chicago and wife. He looked around at the faces of his fellow crewmen staring at the maps, all of them as incredulous as he was with the scope of what deployment meant. Bill felt himself immersed in the comradery, knowing every one of them shared the same thoughts.

The colonel continued, "It's quite a haul and so your B-25s will be equipped with auxiliary fuel tanks to extend your range. Aircraft weight will be pared to the minimum possible. Since you'll be far outside of the enemy's reach, you won't be carrying any ammo, in fact, your planes will be stripped of all guns except for those in the dorsal turret. Crews will likewise be reduced to pilot, co-pilot, navigator, radioman, and engineer."

Someone in a front row raised a hand. The colonel acknowledged him and he asked how the rest of the group was getting across the ocean.

The colonel pointed to South Carolina. "The group and its equipment will board ships in Charleston harbor that will convoy across the Atlantic to Africa."

February 27, 1943

Bill gazed out the window of his B-25 as it descended toward Accra, British Gold Coast. Their formation cruised over the harbor, crowded with ships and boats. He tracked his airplane's shadow as it raced over the water, its dark outline haloed by the sun. The B-25s roared low over the beach, a ribbon of red earth between the turquoise blue of the sea and the intensely green carpet that covered the land. Below, men dragged nets from the surf. Others were busy with tasks on their boats. People looked up from their labors to regard the low-flying bombers. Many of them waved.

Bill found himself waving back, though he knew they couldn't see him. This fleeting connection with other people caused him to think about Betty. As he watched the vista scroll past him, he wondered how he would relate these experiences to his family. What stories would he tell? His adventures crossing the Atlantic would be enough for a lifetime of anecdotes, let alone what excitement waited for him in the upcoming months. Last November the Americans had invaded the coast of North Africa, and so the 321st would soon enter combat.

The B-25s winged over the city of Accra, a jumble of buildings, old and new, crisscrossed by electrical wires. Trucks and animal-drawn carts plodded along the avenues. Clusters of shacks lined the many roads that pierced the jungle. In the fleeting glimpses Bill caught of the people below, he noticed they were all Black, which emphasized the exoticness of the continent and that he and the rest of the Americans were the strangers in this strange land.

One by one, the B-25s touched down on a long grassy strip and followed one another to a parking area. The landing was uneventful. Anticlimactic actually, considering the effort and care required to get here. Which was all right with Bill. They taxied past several aircraft painted in brown and green camouflage and bearing the British blue-white-red roundels, reminding him that this host country was a colony of the United Kingdom.

A row of hangers flanked one side of the airfield, along with an administrative building, complete with control tower and two flag poles, one flying the Stars and Stripes, the other the Union Jack.

When they climbed from their B-25, what first struck Bill was the humidity and hothouse smell. He gulped the thick, moist air and started to perspire as if a tap had been opened under his skin. The crew collected their baggage and by the time they huddled around the pilot, Lieutenant Anderson, the armpits and collars of everyone's coveralls were soaked with sweat.

At the far end of the airfield, a work party was busy extending the runway into the jungle. Much about this location reminded him of the airstrip they had flown out of in Belém, Brazil, which itself had been recently hacked out of the Amazonian jungle.

A small truck painted olive drab motored toward them. Bill didn't recognize the type and took note of the British flag on a placard fixed to the front bumper. The driver, by appearance an enlisted soldier though in a different uniform, hailed them from the cab.

Sgt. Robert Myers, the radioman, nudged Bill. "Look, the steering wheel is on the wrong side."

The driver gave them an impatient wave and groused, "Well, g'on. G'in. The war's not waiting on the likes of you Yanks."

Bill smirked at the driver's English accent and grinned at Myers, "You're going to take that? Being called a Yank? You, a southerner from Birmingham!" Myers grinned back.

They clambered into the rear of the truck and drove past a line of parked bombers to collect more aircrews. By the time they headed toward the group headquarters, men were hanging all over the truck, smoking cigarettes, some standing on the running boards and the rear bumper. The lack of military decorum gave their arrival a festive air, some of the men breaking out in song, "Chattanooga Choo Choo."

They bivouacked in a tent city located within the airfield perimeter. The next days passed in a blur of familiar military activities. Morning formations. Duty rosters. Inspections. Meals were typical army rations, augmented by local coffee which was surprisingly good.

The 321st Bombardment Group was not the only Army Air Force outfit at Accra. Every day brought formations of more twin-engine bombers, some were B-25s, others the sleeker B-26 Marauder, aka the Widow Maker, plus C-47 cargo planes, and dozens of the bigger four-engine B-17 and B-24 heavy bombers, all en route north to the fighting.

Besides taking care of their aircraft, Bill and the other enlisted men of the squadron were issued M-1 rifles and took turns at guard duty. They'd patrol the aircraft parking area and the adjacent hangers. At night, small critters would dash out of the jungle and forage around the airplanes, in complete disregard of the airfield's security procedures. Bill joked to the sergeant-of-the-guard, "Don't they know the rules?"

Bill's favorite post was the guard house by the main gate onto the airfield. During the night, a heavy, barbed-wire gate was dragged across the road. What intrigued him was that every morning, just as twilight started to brighten, local men began to line up along one side of the road. They wore little more than rags. Most were barefoot. They had arrived to work as day laborers to expand the airfield: clearing the jungle, trimming felled trees and converting them to lumber, digging up stumps, and hauling away debris. They were paid ten cents American for a day's work with hot lunch provided. Only the first hundred were hired, and the rest wandered back down the dusty road toward Accra.

In the leadup to the hour to pull the gate back from the road, an assortment of rickety civilian trucks queued up to enter. Each truck brimmed with locals.

"What's with them?" Bill asked. "How come they're not lining up with the others beside the road?" This morning, he stood guard with his British counterpart, a Leading Aircraftman named Bernard Winston.

"Those are contracted work crews," Winston explained. "The airfield negotiates a deal with a local boss who supplies the workers. He collects the money and pays the workers, minus a kickback for his troubles."

Bill shook his head. "Sounds like home."

Winston asked, "What do you mean?"

"Chicago politics."

Of all the cargo the C-47s brought, none was more welcome than the sacks of V-Mail. To preserve space, letters from home were written on special forms that were photographed and rendered as tiny negatives. This way, 1,700 letters, weighing twenty pounds, could be reduced to a 5-ounce roll of film. A photographic detachment at the airfield would print the negatives on sheets of paper, which were cut up into individual letters and sorted into envelopes for delivery. Beside streamlining the logistics, the process eased the tasks of the mail censors. At mail call, Bill received a letter from Betty:

March 3, 1943

Dearest Bill,

Or should I say, DAD. I just returned from the doctor's and he confirmed what I already suspected. Our baby is on the way. Due in August. This is so exciting. Your mother practically exploded with joy when I told her the news. Your sisters are also beside themselves. With the doctor's note I get an extra book of ration stamps. I don't feel much hungrier but everybody at home will enjoy getting a little more in the pantry.

Also, Carl and Florence are expecting their first. He's been given a deferment.

Miss you so much. All is well here, considering Eileen and Pat are suffering with colds. Grammy is doing fine. Marce says hello. We've been busy in the kitchen trying new recipes. Expect a batch of cookies soon. Everyone sends their regards. I've joined the church choir. Besides singing, I get to play the piano. It gets me out of the house and I get to hang around other people doing fun things. It would be nice to know where you are, but you know where I am. Back home waiting for you.

Your loving wife,

Betty

March 10, 1943

Today's guard assignment was at the Accra wharf. Every day, ships shuttled into the harbor, bringing more men and material bound for North Africa, this morning the convoy bringing the rest of 321st was due into the port.

Cargo ships emerged from the distant haze, rectangular shapes that slowly and relentlessly approached the docks.

The escorting warships remained at sea, cruisers to protect the harbor from enemy surface attack while the destroyers circled about like anxious sheep dogs, on the prowl for German U-boats.

As Bill watched the cargo ships maneuver toward the docks, he remembered thinking during the flight from the US, that those sailing across the ocean had the easier time of it. Nothing to do but lounge on the ship, while for him it was a constant worry that they might crash-land in the middle of nowhere, or worse, ditch in the ocean. But now that he was safe on land, he considered that those on the ships lived with a heavier anxiety, almost two weeks sailing through waters infested with enemy submarines and their deadly torpedoes.

Standing on the edge of the pier and with a rifle slung on his shoulder, Bill studied the nearest ship, hoping to glimpse a familiar face among the mass of soldiers gathered along the railings. The gray, slab-sided steamer loomed huge, as big as a city block and just as grimy and stained.

The steamer berthed in slow-motion increments against the pier. The process was a game of tug-of-war with gangs of men who yanked on thick ropes. When the ship was securely lashed against the pier, soldiers emerged by the hundreds down gangplanks, each man hunched beneath a heavy duffel bag. Cranes swiveled over the ship to hoist trucks and enormous slings of cargo. No sooner had an item been placed on the wharf than men would crawl over it, undoing the crane cables. Trucks were immediately driven off. If one didn't start, there was no shortage of men to push it along the pier. Piles of material were likewise attacked by a swarm of stevedores, reducing the pile piece by piece until nothing but the empty sling remained, like ants making short work of a picnic cake.

Other arriving troops included the colored soldiers of the newly created Air Police, armed with heavy weapons and were considered the Army Air Force's infantry, charged with protecting airfields from saboteurs and air and ground attack. To distinguish themselves as the Air Police, their members decorated their helmets with horizontal white stripes and wore small brassards stenciled with the letters, AP.

Myers and Bill observed the unloading of equipment. One of the air policemen circled close and they stood beside one another. Bill felt the urge for conversation but it was Myers who spoke first. He said to the colored soldier. "Must feel like coming home."

The soldier, a corporal, replied, "What are you talking about?"

"Africa?" Myers asked. "You know, where you're from?"

The expression of the corporal's face shifted from bewilderment to irritation. "What do you mean where I'm from? This place ain't nothing like where I'm from."

"Which is where?"

"St. Louis."

Bill elbowed Myers and gave him a look of disgust. "Why do you have to be like that?"

Myers shrugged. "I was just making small talk."

Bill didn't know what to say without feeling like a heel. So he pulled a packet of cigarettes from his pocket, lipped one, and stepped to the corporal. "Got a light?"

The corporal eyed him suspiciously, then dug a brass lighter from his trouser packet and sparked it. Bill lit his smoke, gave it a puff, then offered a cigarette to the corporal.

The corporal tucked the cigarette behind his ear. "I'll smoke it later." He winked. "Thanks."

The plan for the 321st was to not linger in Accra but to head north as soon as possible. First, the B-25s were readied for combat, their equipment brought up to the latest standard and all the machine guns reinstalled. Trucks convoyed material and men to the train station at Achimota, and from there, railroaded into North Africa.

In the meantime, the men were constantly lectured on security, equipment maintenance, sanitation, first aid, and preventing venereal disease. A Royal Air Force flight lieutenant gave a briefing about what to expect in combat. He had piloted an American-made Martin Baltimore, a twin-engine bomber slightly smaller than the B-25, and was a veteran of the battles over the Mediterranean and North Africa. A red-haired man with a thick mustache, he paced in front of easels propping large black and white photos of German airplanes and anti-aircraft guns.

"Don't underestimate the Jerries," he explained. "We've got them outnumbered but they're tough and smart. In the air," he motioned with a pointer to the photo of a fighter plane with a shark-like nose, "your biggest worry is the ME-109. These remain the most numerous." He side-stepped to the next photo, that of a blunt-nosed fighter with a bubble canopy, a sleek tail, and squared-off wings. "However, always keen to pile on the mayhem, the Jerries have introduced their newest fighter, the Focke-Wulf 190. It's fast and heavily armed with two machine guns and four," he emphasized the point by extending four fingers, "20mm cannon." He rocked on his heels. "About the only reassuring aspect about the FW-190 is that they're not very many of them in theater."

Even though it was unlikely the B-25s would tangle with their German bomber equivalents, the flight lieutenant re-viewed the types, all twin-engine: the Heinkel HE-111, the Dornier DO-17, and the excellent Junkers JU-88.

He gestured to another set of photos, these of anti-aircraft guns. "Closer to the ground, the Jerries have all kinds of nas-ty surprises. The most common ack-ack gun is their 20mm Flak-30 or 38. Next up the scale is the 37mm Flak 18. All of these are fully automatic and fairly mobile as they can be carted about on trucks or half-tracks." He pointed to the photo of a large, long-barreled cannon on a wheeled trailer and attended by a squad of men. "This one you've no doubt heard of already, the 88mm Flak 41."

Bill had, unfortunately. The 88 was infamous as the German's most dangerous piece of artillery, able to swat airplanes out of the sky with one ferocious blow. He leaned in to better focus.

The flight lieutenant explained, "It fires a 20-pound shell up to a height of 26,000 feet. The horizontal range is just over nine miles and the rate of fire is 15 to 20 rounds per minute."

The information made the men squirm. The maximum altitude of their B-25s, and one they seldom used, was 24,000 feet, so they couldn't fly above the reach of these guns. The cruising speed of the B-25 was 230 miles per hour, which was just under four miles per minute. A target defended by 88s meant crossing a shooting gallery 18 miles wide. Bill did the math in his head. That meant they'd spend four and a half minutes getting shot at by 88s with each gun hurling at least 60 shells at them in the meantime. Sixty shells times 20 pounds was 1,200 pounds of steel and high explosive blasted upward per gun. Multiply that by however many 88s were on the ground and the airspace above the target would be laced with tons of exploding shrapnel.

Bill's throat went dry. Surviving one attack shrank to calculable odds. Compound that risk by however many missions they'd have to fly, and suddenly, the chances of making it home didn't seem that good.

The lieutenant replaced the photo with the one behind it. This image showed a wrecked 88 in a bomb crater, the gun lying on one side, its mechanism battered and blackened, the various pieces sticking up in random directions like the broken legs of a squashed insect. "I've learned to put things in perspective. You are as deadly to the 88s as they are to you, provided you mind your duties. The enemy is no better or worse than you are. Make sure to put your bombs where they count, and during a low-level raid, strafe the enemy without mercy."

Myers tapped Bill's leg; he offered a cigarette from a packet of Lucky Strikes. Bill took one and nodded thanks. He needed a smoke to calm his nerves. Myers flicked open a Zippo lighter and Bill lit his cigarette from the quivering flame.

The briefing had stripped away the last veneer of complacency from this adventure, revealing in stark detail the grim foundation of their reason to be here, the killing business of war.

Another briefing laid out their deployment north. The next hop would be to Niamey, French Nigeria. Then into the Sahara Desert to an airbase at Ain M'lila, Algeria. And from there, into combat.

9

---◆---

March 20, 1943

Betty answered the door. Bill's younger sister, Eileen, was in the hall. She'd called earlier this morning and said she would stop by. When Betty married Bill, she hadn't thought about how their relationship would extend to his family. What surprised and uplifted her was how supportive her new in-laws were. Florence as her mother-in-law and Eileen as the most doting of the sisters-in-law. And, of course, she had become fast friends with Florence and Carl.

Eileen grinned brightly and ambled in, a large cloth shopping bag weighed her right arm and the valise in her left hand banged against the doorway.

"What's all this?" Betty asked.

As usual, Eileen didn't explain herself. In this regard, she and Bill had a lot in common. They acted on impulse and expected you to catch up. After Eileen stepped into the kitchen and set the bag on the table and the valise on the floor, she glanced at Betty's belly.

Reacting subconsciously, Betty placed both hands over her swollen middle. Well aware that she was starting to show, she still wasn't used to the attention her expanding waistline was getting.

"You've got the day off," she said.

"Of course I do," Eileen replied. "It's Saturday."

Betty sighed. When she found out she was pregnant, she quit her job to stay home. Without the rhythm of a work schedule, she lost track of the days of the week even if she lived with her mom.

"How are you feeling?" Eileen asked.

Betty didn't know how to answer. Physically, she felt pretty good. Emotionally, if she thought about it too much, she could feel overwhelmed. When she first learned she was pregnant, her initial reaction was an intense feeling of being bonded with Bill. She didn't want to get too maudlin about the sensation, but she was carrying their child. They were now a family. No matter what happened to them, she and Bill were two halves of a unique whole, and this child was their special contribution to the world.

And now that she was starting to show, her thinking about the pregnancy had changed focus. Having another human being grow inside you was a miracle. Clearly, all this was happening according to God's plan, so there shouldn't be a mystery to it. But there was a joyful, amazing mystery to the event and what wonders did that...

"Betty?"

She met Eileen's eyes. "Sorry, drifted off for a moment. You'd think with all the time alone I've got lately that I'd give you my total consideration. Seems I get stuck inside my head."

"Understandable," Eileen said. They sat at the table. Eileen pulled two small paper sacks from the shopping bag. "Mom sent these." She lifted one of the sacks. "Chamomile tea for morning sickness." Then lifted the other. "Fennel tea to keep you regular."

"Thanks." Betty resented her digestive problems being the subject of conversation around someone else's table, but she was glad that Florence was looking out for her.

Next Eileen pulled out apples and a box with cake donuts.

"You didn't have to," Betty protested. "Really, I get around on my own. I want to do my own shopping."

"What makes you think these donuts are for you?" Eileen answered, teasing. "Coffee?"

"I'll heat the pot. In the meantime, look." Betty reached for her purse on the table. As she withdrew two ration books her rosary beads spilled out. Betty considered herself as good a Catholic as the next girl, meaning she went to church when could. Lately though, she started carrying her rosary beads and rubbed them whenever she worried about Bill. Betty hurriedly returned the beads to her purse.

Eileen hadn't noticed as she was preoccupied with the ration books. "How did you manage two?"

"The rules say I'm not eligible for more ration stamps even if I am pregnant, but this being Chicago, if you know someone who knows someone . . ." Betty slipped the books back into the purse. "I can get extras of the basics: milk, eggs, flour, meat, butter, soup. Tell me what you want and I'll get it for you."

Eileen gave a sly look.

Betty had the reputation as a straight-shooter but playing loose with the rules was something Bill would've done. Which was why Eileen stopped by so often. Of all of Bill's siblings, Eileen was the closest to him. Then Betty came along, but Eileen wasn't jealous. What really happened was that Bill got yet another admirer in his orbit of admirers. As he used to say, *There's plenty of me for everybody.*

Plus, Eileen was good company who would do what was best for her brother, and that included watching over his wife.

She thumbed through the pile of newspapers sitting on the table and picked one, drawn to a story was about the local Chrysler plant needing more workers to meet war quotas.

"Thinking of changing jobs?" Betty asked. Eileen worked as a clerk with Standard Oil.

"Just seeing what's out there." Eileen laid the newspaper back on the pile. She bent over the valise and clicked open the latches, splaying it open, revealing stacks of neatly folded clothing. "Look what else I brought you." She grasped a blouse and fluffed it. "What do you think? Mom thought you're gonna need some additions to your wardrobe."

The blouse was especially baggy and unfortunately reminded Betty about how big she expected to get. "I'm not sure."

Eileen balled up the blouse and stuffed it into a corner of the valise. "I don't like it either. Wrong color for you." She pulled out another garment and held it high so that it would drape unfolded. It was an olive-drab coverall, even baggier than the blouse.

"That's hideous," Betty exclaimed.

"In case you get hired as a welder."

Betty snatched the coverall and dumped it into the valise, which she snapped closed. "I'll sort through these later. Tell Florence thanks for the clothes. And the tea. Very thoughtful of her."

Eileen touched her hair and then pointed at Betty. "I know a hair dresser who could use some extra money."

"You saying I need my hair fixed?"

"It could use a little here and there."

Betty patted at her curls. "Okay, maybe some trimming. But seeing as I'm pregnant, no one will be looking at my hair."

"It's not for anyone else. It's for you. Don't you feel better about yourself after getting your hair done?"

"That's true." Betty slapped the table and stood. "How about we forget about the coffee and donuts? I'm going stir-crazy. Let's go out for a walk."

After locking up the apartment, she and Eileen rode the trolley to State Street. They walked arm-in-arm along the sidewalk, busy with people taking in a sunny spring day. They passed a line at the butcher shop, then lines at the bakeries, lines for dairy at the grocery stores. Lines everywhere. The rationing system was supposed to prevent shortages, but it seemed that everything was in short supply.

However, these shortages were only an inconvenience for Betty. She still managed to get plenty. While she listened to others grouse about rationing and the demands of the war effort, her thoughts kept gravitating toward Bill and the only thing that she truly wanted, other than a healthy baby, was for his return safe.

Up ahead, a knot of pedestrians blocked the sidewalk. Betty and Eileen circled the packed, little crowd but remained close enough to see what caused the commotion. The center of attention was a young man in a sailor uniform scrambling to stand upright. Apparently he had tripped. Betty wondered why so many people were fussing over him. She raised on tiptoes and craned her neck to see, only to observe that he fumbled with crutches and was missing a leg.

An icy chill poured through Betty. She closed her eyes. With one hand she clasped the collar of her coat, and with the other, gripped Eileen's arm. Eileen stepped off the curb and tugged Betty along to bypass the sailor.

Betty opened her eyes just as Eileen hurried them across the intersection. "Let's go to Wieboldt's. Look around and put our mind on pleasant topics."

Inside the department store, they first stopped at women's clothing and lamented that an austere, military look had crept into fashion. Lots of muted tones and pockets and belts. Proper dress hats and silk undergarments were hardly available.

They lingered in the cosmetics department. Even lipstick was rationed, the companies making the brass lipstick dispensers having been converted to manufacture ammunition cartridges. Perfume was also scarce; those companies now tasked to produce chemicals for military explosives.

Next they decided to visit the upper floors and crowded into the elevator. Along with the other passengers, they furtively scrutinized the operator, a man in his thirties, silently asking themselves, why wasn't he in military service? Too old perhaps. Or that his job as an elevator operator was essential to the war effort? How hard was it to operate an elevator? You move the lever one way to go up. Move the lever the other way to go down. Push one button to open the door. Push the second button to close the door. Memorize the inventory for sale on each floor.

"Mezzanine. Stationery. Books."

"Second floor. Household goods. Furniture."

"Third floor. Gardening. Home repair."

Maybe the guy received a family exemption? Or was he a drunk and couldn't do anything else? Given the boring nature of the job—open the door, close the door, go up, go down—maybe a bottle was what this guy looked forward to at the end of his shift.

When Bill returned from the war, there would be no such dead-end job for him. He had the grit to volunteer for air combat, taking the fight to the enemy and getting this war over with, so Betty had no worries that her husband would come roaring back with ambition.

After spending an hour traipsing the store aisles, they headed back outside, debating on an afternoon matinee. As they continued along the sidewalk, the abrupt chime of bell startled Betty. A young man on a bicycle swerved past, oblivious to how close he had come into colliding with them.

"Hey, watch it!" Eileen shouted.

The rider was a teenage boy, fifteen, sixteen at most, and wore the dark blue uniform of a Western Union messenger. Out the corner of her eye, Betty noticed another flash of blue. A Western Union messenger on foot. And across the street, another messenger on a bicycle. Then another down the street. Whereas earlier she had seen none, now they seemed to be everywhere. Like ants. See one and then there were ants crawling all over the place.

Betty's pace slowed. She focused on the messenger across the street. Slowing his bike, he swung one leg over the seat to dismount. He propped the bike against the wall and repositioned the messenger bag slung over one shoulder. Digging into the bag, he retrieved an envelope, then cross-checked the envelope to the address on the building's façade as if to verify this as the destination for delivery.

Betty envisioned waves radiating from the envelope. Before the war, people welcomed the arrival of a Western Union messenger. At the time, they were mostly college boys, but the war had scooped them up, replacing their ranks with younger teenagers.

Now the appearance of the messenger on a bicycle was a cause for alarm, or dread. They were now no longer bringers of news, good or bad, but of certain disaster and heartbreak. A loved one in the household was now either killed or missing in action, a government euphemism for, *we haven't found the body.*

Betty's heart thumped erratically, increasing into a hammering against her chest. She found herself panting for breath. Her face flushed hot even as the wave of cold panic she had felt earlier returned to electrify her spine with an icy shiver.

She panned her gaze left, then right. The surroundings blurred except for the messengers who remained in sharp relief. They pivoted abruptly toward her and advanced, one arm outstretched, presenting their envelopes and the feared letters within. *We regret to inform you that . . .*

Betty clutched at her throat and felt herself falling inwards, the world dimming and fading to black.

Someone shook her. It was Eileen. "You okay?"

Betty blinked, and the world bloomed with color and fresh air. Cars honked around her. Her gaze looped in all directions, and the messenger boys were all gone.

Finding her equilibrium, she steadied herself. "I'm all right. Just got a little light-headed." She cupped her middle although the pregnancy had nothing to do with her emotional turmoil and hallucinations.

An older man in a business suit and fedora grasped her shoulder and pulled her forward. "Make way for the little lady." He steered her toward the Woolworth's. "Have a seat at the counter and help yourself to a soft drink or a tea." He presented a handful of coins. "My treat."

She waved him off. "No thank you. I appreciate the gesture. I have money."

He made eye contact with Eileen. "You two together?"

Eileen clasped Betty around the middle. "I got her."

The man let go, saying, "Have faith. We're all gonna get through this."

She guided Betty inside the Woolworth's where they sat on adjacent stools along the lunch counter.

Needing to wipe her nose, Betty reached into her coat pocket for a kerchief. Her fingers touched the coins the man had dropped in there, and she drew warm comfort as she remembered his words. *Have faith. We're all gonna get through this.*

That night, when Eileen returned home she readied a blank V-Mail. All day she'd been thinking of Bill and so she decided to write him while her thoughts were still fresh. She refilled her pen with ink and began writing in small, neat print to cram as much as she could into the limited space, dating the letter for tomorrow.

March 21, 1943

> *Dearest Bill,*
>
> *How are you doing? Everyone misses you very much and are always thinking about you.*
>
> *Betty is coming along. I visit her as much as I can which is almost every day. She asked me, joking of course, how much you were paying me to watch her. She stays home tending to the apartment as her mom goes to work. They have a piano that she practices on every day. To relax she says. I wish I could do something so productive to relax. She has a lovely singing voice.*

I visit with the Verwiel's a lot as well. Marce and her brood of tots say hello. You already know that Florence and Carl are expecting. Despite all the people working in the factories, it's getting harder and harder to buy anything. You need ration stamps to buy a birthday cake! We've become experts at reusing everything. We try to look our best but clothing-wise, we are getting a bit shabby. The war production board's solution to ration fabric is to design clothes so ugly hobos wouldn't wear them! Don't write anybody about it, but I'm looking into how I can get involved in all this war excitement. I have a physical scheduled soon. Maybe the Woman's Marine Corps.

I'll keep you apprised on things here in Chicago. We keep a whole row of candles burning for you in the chapel.

Love,

Eileen

10

March 23, 1943

The city of Ain M'lila sat in the middle of a dusty plain. The area reminded Bill of southern California, out toward the Chocolate Mountains east of Barstow. Ain M'lila hadn't been much to begin with, more of a settlement at the junction of two roads and a railhead. Since the war began, the place had swollen in size as a supply depot. Day by day, the train arrived from Accra, having snaked through the heart of Africa, bringing soldiers and tons of equipment.

Because of GIs whose pockets bulged with dollars, Ain M'lila now sprawled beyond its original borders into what was now part slum, part bazaar. Seemed anything was for sale in the dusty warrens: brass trinkets, jewelry, liquor, birds and monkeys, and prostitutes of every skin hue and hair color. Gambling parlors were popular money traps. And with those vices came thieves so sneaky it was rumored they could steal the tires off a Jeep with the guards sitting in it.

Bill preferred to see Ain M'lila from the air.

Bill poured himself a cup of coffee from the pot brewing on the tent's stove. Although they were in Algeria, the weather swung from moderate to icy cold. Snow dusted the tops of the mountains surrounding the airfield. *Snow in the Sahara desert?* Had Bill not seen for himself, he wouldn't have believed it.

This afternoon, however, the weather was agreeable, downright spring-like. The tent flaps were pinned up to let the interior air out. Everyone had returned from their duties at the flight line; now they waited for tomorrow.

Arty Schwartz, one of the other flight engineers, sat on his cot. He was handy with a pencil and presently sketched designs to use as nose art for the squadron's B-25s. Before any painting got done, the group commander had put the word out that the aircraft were not to be decorated until after their first combat mission. Bad luck.

Bill looked over Arty's shoulder at the sketch. It was of Disney's Dumbo. The cartoon elephant had his big ears stretched out as wings. His trunk stuck out straight and was perforated along its length like the cooling jacket of a machine gun. A string of bullets shot out the tip. A bomb was just dropping from between Dumbo's legs. Despite the bellicose details of the vignette—the machine gun and the bomb—the little elephant wore a jolly grin.

Bill set his cup of coffee aside and fished a package of Lucky Strikes from his pocket. He offered a cigarette to Arty, who without interrupting his work, took one. Bill lipped a cigarette for himself, struck a match, and lit their smokes.

Arty flipped through his sketchbook to show his other ideas, *The Buckeye Cannon Ball* and *Southern Belle.* "You nervous about tomorrow?" He was referring to their first combat mission, a high-altitude bombing raid on a supply depot near the coastal port of Bizerte, Tunisia.

"Naw," Bill replied. "It's a milk run." Meaning the target should be lightly defended with no losses expected.

Truth was, he had the jitters same as everyone else. To calm his nerves, he thought about his wife Betty and their forthcoming baby. Like every GI with a girl back home, Bill kept a photo of his sweetheart handy. When he felt low, he'd admire Betty's picture to remind himself how lucky he was to have met her. Though in this photo she looked sleek and trim, by now she'd be showing their baby for sure. It was an effort for him to imagine himself as a father. What kind of life would he provide for his family?

Before he could answer that question, he had to survive this war, and to do that, he had to stay on top of his duties as flight engineer. The details seemed overwhelming; the B-25 was a complex beast. But this was a team effort. The ground crew pulled their weight as did his fellow aircrew, officers and enlisted alike.

"You don't seem too worried," Arty glanced at Bill. "Doesn't anything bother you?"

"Yeah, sure," Bill replied, smiling. "Having to drink army coffee and running out of cigarettes."

"You ever serious?"

Bill pointed to the sketchbook. "You're the one drawing a cartoon elephant."

Before sun up the next day, Bill and the other flight engineers from the squadron were the first through the chow line to gulp down a hearty breakfast of the usual: powdered eggs, toast, coffee, and fried Spam. He smoked a cigarette on the walk to the maintenance hangar where he read updates to the mission (there were none), smoked a second cigarette, then caught a ride on a maintenance truck to the flight line and during the trip smoked a third cigarette. Yeah, despite what he admitted, he was nervous.

The sun peeked over the eastern mountains and bathed Ain M'lila and the airfield in a golden light. Knowing that soon the air would be echoing with the roar of engines, the ambiance seemed strangely quiet and tranquil.

The sign on the edge of the airfield read: *No Smoking. No Open Flames.* Bill and the rest of the smokers in the truck took a final drag, then squashed the cigarettes against the soles of their boots and tossed the butts to the dirt.

The truck slowed behind a row of parked B-25s. The ground crew were already busy going over the aircraft, wiping dew off the canopies and windows, checking for last minute leaks. Bill read the tail numbers and when he saw his aircraft for the day, 41-13181, he called out, "This is mine." The truck slowed for him to hop out the back.

Sergeant First Class Jameson, in charge of the crew chiefs, was under the starboard wing. He clung to the strut of a main landing gear as he stood on the tire. The purpose for these gymnastics was so he could stick his head inside the wheel well of the right-side engine nacelle.

"Any problems?" Bill asked.

Jameson dropped to the ground and wiped his hands. "Looks good."

Bill collected the logbooks from where they rested on a tool stand. The public had the impression that all the aircrews did for maintenance was kick the tires, light the fires, and take off. But every piece of every airplane was subject to volumes of safety regulations and technical bulletins.

He inspected the logbooks (one for the airframe and one for each engine) to verify that all the required maintenance and repairs were signed off as completed. He was certain that Jameson had been thorough but in training, the instructors emphasized that the one time you failed to check another's work, it will be the one time that particular detail had fallen through the crack.

Entry into the B-25 was through a belly hatch just forward of the bomb bay. Bill made his way to the cockpit where he made sure that all switches were off, the controls were locked, and the trim tabs set to "O." He crawled forward to the bombardier's station, then turned around to continue his inspection through the fuselage to the tail. Even though they'd be flying over desert, he made sure the life raft was stowed properly with the jettison handle secured and ready for use.

He then climbed through the dorsal hatch behind the cockpit and clambered on top of the fuselage. He inspected the starboard wing, opening the fuel cell and verifying that the tank was full. He did the same to the port wing.

Bill headed back to the ground. The last place to check was the bomb bay. He inspected the bomb racks and release links, and sniffed for the odor of gas, which would indicate a fuel leak. All looked and smelled okay.

The rest of the crew had arrived and were scrambling off a cargo truck. They'd brought along the aircraft's five machine guns, all oiled and ready. Bill noted their serial numbers in the airframe log book and then they were hefted into the airplane along with cans of ammo. He carried his machine gun to the tail and secured it in its mount. For safety reasons, the guns wouldn't be loaded until they were airborne.

The mission commander and pilot, Lieutenant "Ollie" Olsen, leafed through the logbooks. Meanwhile, Bill counted as the ground crew rotated each of the propellers by hand to pump oil from where it had settled in the lower cylinders.

He greeted a small truck that towed a trailer of six 500-pound bombs. The driver, an ordnance tech, hopped from the truck. He and Bill inventoried the bombs and fuses and noted this in yet another log book. Then the two men removed the nose and tail plugs from each bomb and screwed in the fuses, then attached the arming wire and the shackle. The first bomb was loaded onto a dolly and scooted under the bomb bay. A lifting strap was looped under the bomb and attached to the hoist cables.

Inside the B-25, sergeants Harmer and Mellado—the turret gunner and the radioman—each worked the crank handles on the hoists mounted to the fuselage's spine. Carefully, the bomb was raised into the bomb bay. Bill and the ordnance tech aligned the shackle with the release links until it clicked into place. Bomb secure. That accomplished, they removed the lifting strap and performed the operation five more times until the six bombs resembled olive-green eggs packed neatly in an egg crate. During this entire process, Bill remained focused on his work. One mistake, and they and the airplane would be a smoking crater.

Lieutenant Olsen gathered the crew in front of the aircraft. As pilot, Olsen wore his field cap, the sides bent down in a "fifty mission crush." The other two officers wore garrison caps while the enlisted men donned leather flight helmets.

"All right, boys," Olsen began. "We got a half hour before takeoff. This is it, our first at bat at the Nazis. We'll be in the number four position, in the slot. That means you, Sergeant. O'Loughlin, in the tail, have to really keep your eyes open so that no one crowds against us."

Bill waved. "Count on me, sir."

Olsen ticked down his inspection list. He asked, "Any questions?" Considering how many times they'd gone over every detail of this aircraft and mission, no one had better have a question. After a moment, Olsen clapped his hands. "Let's get to it."

They hustled aboard and buckled into their parachute harnesses. Bill took his place behind Olsen and assisted with the check list. Outside, the fire guard stood with a fire extinguisher in front of the port engine. Olsen's gloved hand hovered by the engine switches just below the instrument panel.

ENGINE START:

Props Clear.

Olsen yelled out his side window. "Clear!"

The fire guard shouted back. "Clear!"

Ignition switches ON.

Booster Pumps ON.

Energize and Prime for 2 seconds.

Engage.

Olsen pressed the Ignition switch for the port engine.

The Wright Twin Cyclone whined and its propeller began to slowly rotate. Then the engine barked, coughing smoke, the propeller pinwheeling. The engine barked again. More smoke. The engine caught and roared. The propeller spun into a blur. The fuselage shook and Bill's guts trembled.

Mixture Control, Full Rich.

Bill read the pressure gauges. He slapped Olsen's shoulder and said through the intercom, "Oil pressure, 40 pounds. Okay."

Booster pumps, OFF.

Fuel pressure, 6-7 lbs.

Engine RPM, 1200.

Hydraulic pressure, *check*. Brake pressure, *check*. Manifold Suction, 3.9 inches Hg, *Check*.

Radio ON.

Olsen gave a thumbs up to the fire guard. He nodded and dragged the fire extinguisher to the starboard engine to repeat the procedure.

When Bill looked up, dozens of propellers flashed in the sunlight. Olsen waved his hand out the side window. Two of the ground crew ran at diagonals from under the wings, each man holding a pair of yellow wheel chocks.

Olsen said, "Everybody to takeoff positions."

Bill settled into his seat behind Olsen's, facing aft, listening to the intercom buzz through his headphone, feeling his insides quiver like jelly. The airplane remained in place, waiting its turn. Then the B-25 taxied forward and pivoted gently. Olsen had a light touch on the controls. By peering out the side window, Bill saw the group of aircraft ambling into file like a herd of well-trained beasts.

When they reached the runway, the B-25 eased to a halt. The engines shrieked. When the brakes were released, the bomber rolled forward, gaining speed, rumbling louder, louder, until Bill felt his body lift, his abdomen pressing against bottom of his pelvis. They continued straight, climbing.

"All right boys," Olsen said, "everybody get to your positions. Load your guns."

Bill uncoupled his intercom. With the airplane swaying around him, he made his way to the tail. Harmer had scrunched down to climb into the dorsal turret. Mellado was framed against a side window. Near the tail, Bill shrugged out of his parachute harness and jammed it into a nook between the ammo cans and the fuselage. He dropped to his knees and crawled into the tail cone. He lay on his belly.

Before loading his gun, he checked to make sure that the weapon was not pointed at another airplane in the formation. All clear.

He performed the familiar ritual of loading the gun. Feed tray cover open. Align the belt of ammo in the feed tray, close the cover. Yank hard on the charging handle until the gun was loaded and ready. Verify the safety.

He connected to the intercom and heard, "Turret loaded."

"Nose guns loaded."

Bill added, "Tail gun loaded."

Olsen said, "Okay boys, test fire. Let 'em rip."

The airframe reverberated from the staccato blasts of the guns. Bill grasped the spade grips of his machine gun and aimed into empty sky. When he depressed the trigger, the gun bellowed. Tracer bullets arced toward the horizon.

"Tail gun ready."

They cruised north and low over the desert. Bill observed the trailing bombers tuck close. Looking down, he regarded their shadows, the six bombers of his squadron in a tight formation resembling the point of a spear.

So far, the mission seemed routine enough. They flew on a steady course for several minutes, then banked to a new heading, repeating this process several times as they zigzagged to disguise their route to the target.

The desert was hardly uniform. Gray outcroppings of rocky escarpment cut through the broad swaths of beige sand. The few oases were not like those in the picture books: aqua pools of water ringed by tall palms but were rather muddy puddles surrounded by scraggly thickets.

Bill kept his eyes open. No one had consulted with the enemy as to whether they agreed that this mission would be a "milk run." The Germans hadn't gotten this far by being push-overs.

The formation began a slow turn to the east, climbing to 10,000 feet. Olsen said anxiously, "Okay boys, we're over the IP." The *Initial Point*, from where they started their attack run.

Bill detected a palpable tension not only from the other crew but from all the aircraft. The bombers inched closer, locking into a steady, tight formation.

He kept watch on the trailing B-25s. Bomb bay doors cranked open. *Any second now.* When the lead airplane dropped its bombs, that was the signal for the group to un-leash their deadly cargo.

Bill's pulse thumped hard. He forced himself to breathe deeply. The enemy was directly below. At any moment, the immediate sky would be black from exploding 88s.

On cue, every bomber dumped its load. Bill followed the bombs as they fell, shrinking to dots, then disappear-ing against the backdrop of open desert. Tents and parked trucks—toy-like because of the distance—straddled a road that scrolled into view. The enemy depot. For a long mo-ment nothing seemed to happen.

Then explosions rippled along the road, flashing yel-low and orange, then darkening into blossoms of smoke. Considering the tight formation, Bill expected the bombs to cluster right across the tents. But bombs exploded all over the place, many of them landing in empty desert.

A second string of explosions tore through the tents, shooting up gouts of fire. Trucks disappeared, only to reappear as flaming wrecks. At least some of the bombs found their mark.

The depot receded behind them, tall flames weaving into clouds of black smoke. Bill keyed the intercom mike, "Tail gunner to pilot. Bomb damage assessment. Maybe fifty percent hits on target."

Though they were leaving the target, Bill couldn't let himself relax. The air should be filled with enemy flak. Yet nothing.

Harmer said, "I think they're asleep down there."

Mellado added, "Don't they know there's a war on?"

Harmer rejoined, "That should wake 'em up."

The B-25 banked and the Mediterranean tilted into view. The blue expanse was a fantastic sight juxtaposed against so much desert wasteland. Dust clouds rose from the ragged strips of green along the coastline. Out in the water, ships dragged white wakes.

Minute by minute, the bombers pulled south and the Mediterranean flattened into a blue line, then became a gray haze, then vanished all together over the horizon.

Bill thought, *Wow! That was easy.* But he didn't speak it. Didn't want to jinx the ride home. Afterall, this was only their first combat mission.

William (Bill) O'Loughlin's First Holy Communion 1926

Bill and Sisters: Marcelline, Florence, Eileen and Patricia. Circa 1925

Bill's High School Graduation: Circa 1935

Bill in Illinois National Guard Uniform: Circa 1939

Ruth Elizabeth Cummings
(Betty)

Weapons Training: Location unknown

Carl Ladwig and Bill at Ladwig Wedding: July 12, 1941

Bill and Betty at Ladwig Wedding: July 12, 1941

July 12, 1941: Bill with Virgie, Bill's Mother Florence, Bill's sister Florence, Eileen, Patricia, (male unknown)

Bill and Eileen: July 1941

Betty, Florence, and Carl: Photo Presumably Taken by Bill

Bill and Betty Wedding Day Photo, South Carolina: August 30, 1942

Bill O'Loughlin: Date/location unknown

Bill on his way to mission preparation. Foggia Italy

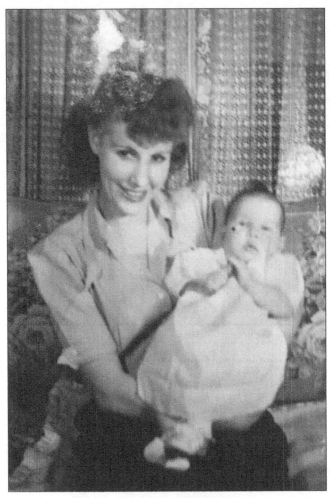

Betty and Maureen 1943

Bill, Foggia Italy

Bill (upper right) and partial crew of the SNAFU: Foggia, Italy

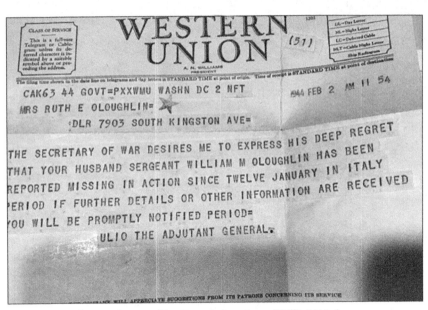

Telegram Received by Betty informing of Bill's MIA Status

Chicago Press Clipping; February 1944

A SOLDIER'S PRAYER
At Taps and Reveille

+

O God of power and love, behold me before Thee this night (morning) to add my faltering prayers to those which a little child daily brings to Thee in my behalf.

Make me a soldier (sailor, Marine) worthy of the great cause for which we fight.

Give me strength when the going is hard.

Give me courage when danger is near.

In Thee I place my trust. Lead me through the perils of this war to the peace of that better world to which I have dedicated my life. But if the service of Thee and my Country calls for the sacrifice of my life, I only ask, dear God, that Thou be with me at that moment, confident that Thy peace awaits me in eternity.

AMEN.

H. B. LAUDENBACH,

Censor Librorum

Imprimatur: JOHN A. DUFFY

Item from Bill's footlocker

Artist's rendering of the WWII B-25, Buckeye Canon Ball, being shot down on January 12, 1944 in Italy near the Isoleta Dam depicting the pilot, 1st Lt. Frederick William Vincent III, USAAF, being ejected from the blast. Lt. Vincent parachuted into a German Camp and was take as a Prisoner of War to Stalag Luft 1 Prison Camp

Isoletta Dam 2017

11

---◆---

April 4, 1943

Bill's B-25 roared over the desert. Today he was in aircraft 42-64600, sporting its new nose art as *Lady Luck*.

From his vantage in the tail, Bill studied the squadron's bombers as they swayed and banked to remain in formation. Swiveling his head from side-to-side, he could see the big twin rudders and the elevators to his left and right make minute adjustments as the pilot and copilot manipulated *Lady Luck's* controls. It seemed incredible that it was men inside who operated this big flying machine. Watching the airplanes cruise through the sky, it was almost possible to believe that they flew themselves.

The group raced over the mountains. P-40 fighters followed behind them, high and to the left and right, ready to interfere with any enemy interceptors.

Smoke rose from a distant valley. Operational security dictated that the aircrews were briefed with only enough information to accomplish their mission. The reason was that should any of them have to bail out and then get captured, they couldn't reveal what they didn't know.

But scuttlebutt filled in the blanks between what Bill and the rest had been told. A few weeks ago, in their first crack at the Germans, American ground units had taken a pasting at a place called Kasserine Pass. Since then, II Corps had been reorganized, the commander sacked, replaced by a firebrand Bill never heard of, some general named George Patton.

Now the American air units were closely tied to support a ground offensive around another patch in the desert called El Guettar. Specifically, the 321st was to hit enemy reinforcements spotted on the road between Faid and the coastal town of Sfax.

When in public school, Bill had never been one for geography. At the time, all that mattered was how to get around Chicago. Then when he'd enlisted in the Illinois National Guard, he'd gotten to travel around the US. After the war started, he joined the Army Air Force and that further broadened his appreciation of the American continent. Now overseas, he'd study maps to comprehend his place in the Big Picture. Two years ago, he would've dismissed anyone who told him he'd be flying over North Africa and living in and fighting over places he could barely pronounce as totally wacko.

The buzz in Bill's headset interrupted his thoughts. "Everyone there?" It was the copilot, Lieutenant Davis. "Sound off."

One by one, the crew at their various positions replied. "Bombardier." "Radioman." "Turret gunner."

Bill keyed his intercom. "Tail gunner."

For this mission they flew without a navigator or photographer.

Davis didn't say anything more. Chatter in the airplane was kept to a minimum, and Davis probably made the request to make sure everyone remained awake and that the intercom was working.

Several minutes passed. The B-25 tipped abruptly to starboard. Bill felt his guts sway inside his belly. The bombers behind replicated the maneuver. Bill glanced at his watch and regarded the change in terrain, rugged mountains flowing into smoother hills. They must be passing the final inbound checkpoint to the IP. Bill's pulse notched up.

Then when the hills flattened into a ragged plain of escarpment, the pilot, Lieutenant Jahraus, announced, "We're over the IP." *Lady Luck* banked to port. A road two thousand feet below angled into view. Holding steady over the road, the squadron pulled tight, each aircraft nudging closer, closer still, until Bill could read the anxious expressions of the bombardiers in the nose greenhouses and the pilots behind their windscreens.

"I wanna see a tight pattern on the target," Colonel Knapp, the group commander, had demanded in the premission briefing.

Bill imagined the attack unfolding. The P-40 escorts would divide into three elements. The first element would strafe the target and get the flak guns to open up and reveal themselves. The second element would take out the flak guns and clear the way for the bombers. The third element would remain as top cover should enemy fighters show up.

When he felt *Lady Luck's* bomb bay doors open, he coughed to clear his throat. *Getting close.* To calm his nerves, he reviewed how he and the ordnance tech had attached the six 500-pound bombs inside the bomb bay. Fuses, *check.* Arming wires, *check.* Shackles, *check.* Release links, *check.*

Then he sensed the *click, click, click* of each successive pair of bombs released. Simultaneously, clusters of bombs dropped from the other B-25s.

At the instant the bombs appeared, Bill could swear he could see the small propellers on the nose fuses whirl, that's how close the airplanes were to each other. He watched the bombs fall, arcing downward like a well-ordered swarm of bees.

Explosions straddled the road, obscuring the target with dust and smoke. Fireballs twisted upward—direct hits on vehicles. Tiny dots—men—sprinted from the road. Trucks, tanks, and half-tracks swerved into the desert, throwing rooster tails of dust.

Bill tallied the destruction and keyed the intercom. "Tight pattern on the road. Two fuel trucks hit. Counted five direct hits on tanks and other trucks."

The B-25 nosed downward to gain speed and veered to port. Bill scooted farther into the tail cone to keep a visual on the target. P-40s zoomed over the road.

Lieutenant Jahraus announced, "On to secondary target." After they had dumped their bombs on the primary target, the group was to attack any other enemy units caught in the open.

"What's the target?" Lieutenant McCormick, the bombardier, asked.

"We got word of another column heading this way," Jahraus answered. "Gonna rough 'em up a bit. No sense retuning home with all this ammo."

The B-25s wheeled into a loose trail formation, banking sharply to show off their broad wings. For a strafing run, the planes were to string out at odd intervals to make it harder for the flak gunners to draw a bead.

The ground rose toward them. Bill tightened his grip on his machine gun's spade grips as the terrain raced away from him. He noted that he was fighting the war going backwards.

Lady Luck's forward machine guns chattered. The turret guns added to the chorus.

The ground swelled into view, filling in the vista seen through the tail cone. Balls of fire and smoke clotted the air.

Thump! Thump!

Lady Luck had taken two hits. A string of white tracers snaked toward Bill. He fixed his sight at the source of the tracers and fired, the machine gun shaking. The road and the panorama of flame and ruin shrank into the distance. Bill released the trigger. Acrid smoke from the hot gun stung his eyes. He wiped them with the back of his glove.

"We got a couple holes in the fuselage," Dexter the radio-man said, appraising the damage. "Just added to the ventilation, that's all."

Bill sighed, grateful that *Lady Luck* should make it back to base. One more mission down. Hopefully, one more mission closer to home.

April 5, 1943

Bill stared at the V-Mail form, frustrated that he had so much to tell but limited in what he could write. The form offered only an abbreviated space for his message and he had to be careful in what he wrote to get it past the censors.

Here he was in the middle of his life's greatest adventure and all he could say was, *We're doing fine. The food could be improved. Appreciate your last letter.*

He chastised himself for not thinking through this letter-writing task more thoroughly. Some of the other guys had devised a code with their sweethearts to divulge more than the usual. One method was to have the first letter in a sentence spell out where you are. Another was to have decided upon code words like pigs for trucks, sparrows for airplanes, something like that.

For the sake of keeping up morale back home, war losses were a taboo topic. What was on Bill's mind was his thoughts of watching the group's first bomber get blown out of the sky. A direct hit from an 88 during a raid on Tunis. One moment the B-25 was holding station at the left rear of the formation. Then it was swallowed in a clap of flame and smoke. The bomber tumbled downward, breaking apart, each piece trailing fire and smoke. Bill watched in horror, hoping to see at least one parachute, but nothing. The pieces spun out of view and just like that, six men were no more.

The image kept looping through his memory, but what he settled on was this letter to his sister Eileen.

Dearest Eileen,

Hey Sis, thanks for your last letter. You can't imagine how welcome these notes from home are. How are you? Betty? Thinking about you keeps my mind off the war. Then thinking about the war keeps my mind off how much I miss you all. You asked about army chow. Here's the good and bad. The good, we have so much of it. The bad, we have so much of it. The Arabs are smart enough not to eat Spam until we tell them it's not pork and instead mutton, and then they gobble it up! Sooner or later this war will be over and I'll see all your smiling faces. And what's this business about the Women's Marine Corps? I'd

like to not tell anyone about it but that might be difficult. The
"excitement" isn't all it's cracked up to be, trust me. You're lucky
I'm not home.

   Love, Bill

May 15, 1943

The last of the Germans and Italians in North Africa had
surrendered. *Good news, I suppose,* thought Bill. Not that the
war was anywhere close to over. The Allies were pressing forward with the offensive, using Sicily as a stepping stone for
the invasion of Italy.

In a rare form of disclosure to the rank and file of the
Twelfth Air Force, the Allied Command announced the
start of Operation Corkscrew. It's mission was to take out
the Italian defenders on Pantelleria and Lampedusa, two island outposts 140 miles south of Sicily. The Italians operated radar that provided forewarnings of Allied air and ship
movements and they aimed big guns that could threaten any
passing ships.

Besides bombing the islands directly, the plan for Operation
Corkscrew was to isolate them by attacking any resupply con-
voys. To that end, a reconnaissance aircraft had spotted a small
flotilla departing Marsala, on course to Pantelleria. The 321st
was ordered to intercept, attack, and destroy.

Though the B-25 was designed as a torpedo bomber, aircrews in the Pacific reported that the Mark 13 torpedoes were worse than useless. Instead, those units introduced "skip bombing," where 500-pound bombs were dropped at high speed from low level, typically between 200 and 250 feet, and allowed to skip across the water like stones. The bombs were fitted with five-second delay fuses to allow the aircraft time to escape. Provided the attack was pressed with bravado and precision, the success rate was close to a hundred percent.

But the technique was not without its hazards. One of which was that the bomb could explode upon striking the water right under the bomber, or the bomb might bounce back up into the bomber, or the bomb might skip completely over the target ship. And the greatest hazard of all was that the B-25s would be attacking straight into the barrels of the ship's flak guns.

But the idea of taking the fight to the enemy face-to-face ignited a pugnacious spirit within the men of the 321st. They were young, adventurous, and audacious.

Thirty minutes after take-off, the twenty-four B-25s were in formation over the Mediterranean, cruising at ten thousand feet in a wide clockwise maneuver around Pantelleria. Two squadrons of P-38s provided cover should enemy fighters make their appearance. The rocky island was a blot on the horizon, smudged by smoke from aerial and ship bombardment.

Bill surveyed the enormous breadth of the Mediterranean, taking in the sight with amazement. The sea was a deep blue-green, the color of an exotic carpet. Chagrinned by the wonder the musings brought, here he was flying over the same waters plied by the Phoenicians, the ancient Greeks, and the Romans.

"Targets ahead," the pilot, Lieutenant Joiner, said, bringing Bill to the present. "Five cargo steamers and a couple of patrol boats."

The group's squadrons separated into four attack elements. Bill was by now familiar with the routine. The elements would attack from different directions to keep the enemy guessing. For this mission he was tail gunner of the squadron's lead aircraft, 42-64546 *Jessie James*. This gave him the perfect vantage to observe the squadron array itself for the attack. A year ago in training, these same bombers lumbered through the air like a gaggle of clumsy geese. Now they readied themselves like giant hawks, keen to pounce upon the enemy and annihilate them.

For skip bombing, the B-25s carried four bombs instead of the usual six. Practice had shown they could only pickle four bombs, dropped in pairs, with the certainty of hitting the target. The first two bombs were skipped and the second pair slammed point-blank into the enemy ship. Carrying two extra bombs only added weight for the sudden maneuvering required when breaking off the attack run.

The bombers entered a wide, descending turn to port. Bill watched his squadron's six aircraft spread out in a loose line. Every pilot was free to maneuver on his chosen target. Lower and lower the B-25s flew, their shadows racing beneath them on the water.

Like raptor's talons, bomb bay doors snapped open.

White tracers zipped past. The enemy wasn't going down without a fight.

Jessie James's forward machine guns opened up to answer the ship's defenses. More tracers tore through the air.

Then, *click, click. Bombs away.*

Jessie James nosed upward and banked sharply. Centrifugal force pressed Bill against the aircraft deck.

The ship flashed beneath him. Fountains of water splashed upward. Bill ripped loose a good burst, watching his bullets spray and ricochet off the ship's hull. Then explosions, huge blossoms of flame that tore open the deck. Concussive blasts rocked the *Jessie James.*

"Four hits!" Bill shouted.

A second B-25 closed in, unleashing a torrent of machine gun tracers that splattered across the enemy ship, now on fire. Four bombs dropped, two by two. Geysers. Explosions.

Jessie James soared upward, the squadron in tow. Bill squirmed to get a better view of the attack. All five of the enemy cargo ships were dead in the water, smothered by fire and smoke and surrounded by burning oil. Falling debris peppered the water. Though the enemy was done, the fourth squadron of the group was approaching in attack formation, ready to deliver the coup de grâce.

"Turret gunner, get ready," Lieutenant Joiner sang out. "Patrol boat to port."

"Roger," answered Manning.

Patrol boats were too small and nimble to bother attacking with bombs. Instead the B-25s would single out a boat and orbit above it, letting the turret gunners fire broadsides to chop the wooden craft into flaming pieces. To Bill the technique reminded him of a western movie where the Indians would surround a covered wagon, galloping in a circle as they riddled the pioneers with arrows.

At first the patrol boats fought back as if they were cornered rats, baring their machine guns and automatic 20mm cannon like fangs. But under the withering barrage of .50 caliber bullets funneled upon them, the enemy's guns fell silent, the crews minced into bloody rags.

The bow of the patrol boat slipped into the water. Sailors jumped clear. The fight was over. Bill wanted to shout, *Cease fire!* But orders were to continue an attack until the enemy was destroyed or you ran out of ammunition.

Tracers bullets rained nonstop upon the hapless patrol boat. Then it fire-balled, and what was left remained swamped in the water, smoldering and slowly disappearing.

The B-25 banked level, and the turret guns fell silent. The squadron followed *Jessie James* out of the turn, on course for home.

Below, the enemy sailors splashed toward one another, tiny dots of humanity struggling to remain alive. In any other situation, Bill's duty would've been to help rescue them. Now, it was to let them die. This was war without mercy.

12

August 18, 1943

Betty rinsed the last of the breakfast dishes and returned to the kitchen table. Her mother had already left for work. In these quiet moments all to herself, Betty prepared herself for the day. Shortly, she'd step outside and shop for pastries and perhaps a newspaper. For the last two weeks, as her due date approached—actually, it was any day now— she had prepared everything for the sudden departure. *When labor starts*, her mother had cautioned, *it can come quick!* Betty's bag was packed with every possible item that she'd need, from toothpaste to fresh undergarments, to slippers. The issue had been to not overpack. After all, it wasn't like she was going overseas to have the baby.

This afternoon, Eileen would stop by and together they'd go for a stroll. Betty rubbed her immensely round belly. She surprised herself as to how mobile she remained. Walking was good exercise her doctor had emphasized. Though she had gained a hefty twenty-five pounds, Betty was certain that in short order after the birth, she'd get her figure back. The women in her family were naturally disposed that way and during the pregnancy, she hadn't gotten into the habit of binge eating.

She felt the baby move and lovingly cupped both hands over her abdomen. Thoughts of Bill returned and she imagined his face practically exploding with glee when he would eventually set his eyes on his child.

Boy or girl? Betty kept rubbing her belly and wondering.

She retrieved the folder where she kept Bill's letters and slipped out the one on top. It was his most recent and she began reading.

August 2, 1943

Sweetheart,

If I said I missed you, that would be the biggest understatement of the war. I'd give anything to see you right now, before the baby is born. Make sure to send pictures as soon as you can. How are Pat and Marce? Tell Eileen her biscuits would be a hit over here. I've learned a lot since being in the army. I used to think I knew what bad food tasted like but the army proves that it's the expert at making our stomachs churn. I think instead of bombs, we ought to drop on the enemy the "meatballs" the chow-hall served the other night. The war would be over quick. Our biggest battle so far is against the sand fleas that are making life Holy Hell. The other night we watched the movie "Girl Crazy."

A lot of the guys were hooting for Judy Garland. If she dropped by for a visit, she'd have no shortage of partners on her dance card. Hope everyone at home is doing great. Despite my complaining, I'm a soldier after all (a soldier who's not complaining is either sick or up to no good) actually I'm doing alright. Just wishing this war would hurry up and end so I could get back to the important things in life like being with you and our baby. Give my regards to everybody.

Love,

Bill

August 19, 1943

A sudden pain woke Betty. The source of the pain was an intense cramp in her lower back that came in waves, tightening, then relaxing, then tightening again with greater pressure. She rolled out of bed and reached for the robe draped over an adjacent chair. After slipping into the robe, she forced herself to shuffle across her darkened bedroom.

She was due but remembered how her doctor had warned about false labor. She grasped her waist just above her hips and massaged her lower back. Pacing back and forth in her room, she analyzed the discomfort, becoming increasingly certain that she was, indeed, in labor.

The baby kicked. Hard. Betty clasped her belly and tracked the pointed edges of the baby's bones as they skimmed across the inside of her womb.

Now she felt an intense desire to pee and hurried for the bathroom. Once in the hall, she heard a click from her mother's bedroom. A thin light outlined the door. Her mother padded out of bed and approached the door, opening it.

"Is it time?" Ruth cinched a robe, backlit from a lamp on the nightstand.

"I don't know," Betty whispered. Emotions tumbled through her. Anxiety over the pain. Fear of what the delivery would be like. Apprehension about the health of the baby. Anticipation that this burden would be finally over.

"How bad is the pain?"

"Nothing I can't handle." Betty continued to the bathroom and flicked the light switch, blinking at the abrupt glare reflecting off the mirror and tiles.

A moment later she returned to the bathroom's doorway and said to her mother. "We better go. It's time."

"Are you sure?"

"Quite sure. My water just broke."

Each moment of the delivery came to Betty in distinct, sharp-focus clarity, only to rush by and get lost in the blur of memory. The singular event that remained etched in her mind was the one where she was lying on her back on the delivery table, the icy sensation of the stirrups cupping her bare heels, the overhead lamp shining as bright as the sun but giving no warmth, the sense of monumental exertion and pain centered in her lower abdomen, her sister Shirley—a nurse in the hospital—squeezing her hand.

Then, the cry of a baby and the doctor's voice announcing, "It's a girl."

And with that, the pain ebbed. She tried lifting her head to see the baby but Shirley pushed her shoulder against the table. "Don't move. Let yourself rest."

Another nurse, an older woman with dark hair pinned under her cap, clasped each of Betty's ankles and tenderly lifted her legs from the stirrups as Shirley helped Betty scoot up the table. They covered her naked hips and legs with a sheet. Betty reflected on what her mother had told her: *There is no dignity in child birth.* Wasn't that the truth.

Betty struggled to sit up. Her hair hung in damp strands, moist with the sweat of exertion. The baby's wail echoed in the delivery room. Betty searched for a glimpse of her infant, now cradled in Shirley's arms. She lay the baby on the scales, noted the weight, then swaddled the baby in a flannel blanket and brought the bundle to Betty.

The wave of emotions surprised her. First, exhaustion. Then surprisingly, pride. An intense feeling of accomplishment, that she alone had brought this tiny human being into the world.

Betty held the pink child to her chest. Its face was fading from red to pink. Wisps of pale hair curled from the little round head. The baby settled warm and soft to Betty's bosom.

What came to mind was the baby's name. *Maureen.*

Love as she had never felt before swirled over and through Betty. A selfless love, not of desire, but of an intense motherly longing and concern. From now until Betty died, this child would be at the center of her life.

And her life with Bill. Bringing a baby to this world had been an ordeal. But even now, minutes after all the pain and anxiety, if Bill had told her that he wanted another mouth to take care of, she would've eagerly said yes.

How many children? If they brought as much pleasure as this new one, then as many as she and Bill could afford.

Pulling baby Maureen tight to her breast, Betty let herself ease into a dreamy future. Toddlers running through their house. The kitchen filled with the aroma of pot roast and warm bread. Bill admiring her with his slick, charming smile. He was as sincere in his affection for her and she was with him.

However, worries remained to mar this vision. After all, he was on the other side of the world, defying the odds with every flight into harm's way. But with tiny Maureen so warm and vulnerable against her, Betty wouldn't change a thing. This baby represented the future, a future with the three of them, Bill, Maureen, and Betty.

Someone called to her.

Betty blinked and the pleasant musings vanished like mist.

The man repeating her name was Dr. Gustafson. He regarded her from where he was hunched over a table against the wall. He was a haggard-looking middle-aged man. Betty was one of three deliveries he had tended since midnight so he had every right to appear like he'd been through the wringer. A surgical cap sat askew on his broad forehead and miscolored stains spattered the white apron draped over his doctor's smock. He held a pen and said, "Maureen O'Loughlin," to confirm the baby's name for the birth certificate.

Betty slid her fingers into the blanket and stroked the infant's pliant skin. "Yes. Maureen O'Loughlin."

Eileen was staring at her reflection in the bureau mirror as she brushed her hair. Florence, her mother, and Patricia, her younger sister, were in the kitchen, fixing breakfast.

The phone rang, its abrupt chime interrupting the rhythm of the morning's activities. Eileen tracked Florence's steps rushing to the phone, Patricia at her heels, answering on the third ring. Eileen glanced to the clock on her night-stand. 7:15. Anyone who called at this early hour could only be bringing urgent news.

She held her breath to eavesdrop on the call. Her mother chatted in an increasingly loud and happy tone. When the phone clattered back into its cradle, Eileen leaned into the hall to learn the cause of the excitement.

Radiant with joy, Florence clapped her hands, exclaiming, "That was Ruth. Betty gave birth to a baby girl."

"Wow," Patricia said. "This family sure is getting big."

True, noted Eileen. Their oldest sister, Marcelline, already had five in her brood and was again several months pregnant.

"What's the baby's name?" asked Patricia.

"Maureen," answered Florence.

Eileen gathered her things into a purse. "Where is Betty?"

"Evangelical Hospital."

Eileen rushed to the phone and asked the operator to connect her to the main office of Standard Oil. Julie, the morning receptionist, answered.

Eileen exchanged pleasantries then said, "Take a note for Mr. Halderman." He was her boss. "Tell him I've got a family emergency and I'll be in around noon." Eileen sorted through her day's tasks. War or no war, she had more impor-tant things to do this morning.

After hanging up, she hustled into the kitchen and col-lected a cloth grocery bag and a small empty Thermos. She paused by the mirror along the front door and gave herself one last once-over to make sure she looked presentable.

"Where are you off to?" Patricia asked.

"To see your newest niece." Eileen headed out.

Evangelical Hospital sat on a grassy, elevated slope at the corner of South Morgan Street and 54th Place, several blocks east of Sherman Park. The hospital had been established by the Evangelical Church of Chicago to provide an orphanage, home for the elderly, and an infirmary. The orphanage and home had since been moved elsewhere but the infirmary remained, having evolved into a hospital, which welcomed anyone regardless of denomination, including Catholics. Eileen had often donated money to one of the neighborhood Ladies Auxiliaries who helped keep the hospital going. Little had she realized then that she might be visiting relatives within those same walls.

Eileen found Betty on the second floor of the hospital. Betty rested on a bed, one of many women patients in the open ward. The privacy curtain around Betty's bed had been pushed back. Eyes closed, she lay propped on pillows, appearing very tired but content.

A blonde about her age, wearing a wrinkled nurse's uniform sat in the chair beside Betty's bed. She was leaning over Betty, whispering, smirking like she was sharing a joke.

Upon Eileen's approach, Betty opened her eyes a crack, then discovering it was her sister-in-law, she tried to sit up, only to wince in discomfort.

"Easy," the nurse soothed.

Betty relaxed. She extended a hand from under the bedcovers and pointed to the nurse. "Eileen, this is my sister, Shirley."

Eileen had heard mention of Shirley before but hadn't met her. They exchanged greetings, Shirley saying, "Thank you for coming by."

Eileen made an obvious gesture of searching for the baby. "Where's Maureen?"

"In the nursery to give Betty a break," Shirley answered. "The baby is so beautiful. All ten fingers and toes." She read her wrist watch. "I better get back to my rounds." She kissed Betty on the cheek, then rose from the chair, nodding goodbye to Eileen as she left.

Eileen scooted the chair against the bed and sat. She presented a small paper sack from her grocery bag. "I brought you crullers. One plain, the other chocolate."

Betty pushed up onto the pillows. "Thanks. I'm famished. They gave me some orange juice but said I had to wait for lunch."

Eileen lifted the Thermos from the bag. She unscrewed the cap, uncorked the container, and poured coffee into the cup. "Loaded with cream and sugar the way you like it."

Betty brought the cup to her nose and inhaled the leaf of steam. "Smells wonderful."

"You look exhausted."

"I am. And very sore."

"Still planning for a big family?"

Betty chuckled, then sipped the coffee. Her eyes narrowed in delight as she savored the warm brew. "I'm sure the topic will come up when Bill returns home."

Eileen appreciated her sister-in-law's upbeat attitude.

Betty perched the cup on the nightstand's corner. "Any news?"

"About what?"

Betty reached for the paper sack and fished out the plain cruller. "About anything. New developments. Gossip."

While Betty tore the cruller in half and dipped one broken end into the coffee, Eileen thought about what interesting tidbits she could share. Trouble was, she and Betty had spent yesterday afternoon together and nothing noteworthy had happened since then.

"I brought this." Eileen dipped into her bag and brought out a fresh V-Mail. "I'll let you be the first to break the good news to Bill."

Betty took the V-mail. "I'm glad you thought of this."

"Do you have a pen?"

Betty glanced to her overnight bag shoved under the nightstand. "It's in my purse."

"Is there anything you want? You need?" Eileen asked. "The other girls and me have taken up a collection."

"Let me think about it," Betty answered. "I already have the baby. So what I really need is Bill."

13

August 30, 1943

"All right," Lieutenant McFadden said over the intercom, "shut the engines."

As Bill read from the checklist, McFadden and the co-pilot, Lieutenant Langston, cut the power. Static hummed through the headset. Their aircraft, 41-30557, had been the spare for the day's mission. That meant the crew had gone through every aspect of the mission prep, including loading bombs. But the other six bombers had taken off without a hitch and were now specks shrinking into the distance, high above the dusty, wind-swept airfield at Soliman in Tunisia.

Bittersweet relief washed over Bill and his fellow crewmen. Not going was a reprieve from the risks of another mission. Yet not going also meant that they had to fly another day to complete their combat tours. Calculating the odds for either occurrence was an exercise in futility. Today's operation could be a disaster, a flight straight into a gauntlet of hungry flak guns and Messerschmitt fighters. Or it might be the smoothest of milk runs.

Bill was glad they didn't go. He had other things to think about besides flying and war.

After the engines shut down, and while the rest of the crew was trucked back to operations, he remained behind to supervise the unloading of the bombs and signing them over to the ordnance techs. *Wouldn't that take all,* he reminded himself, *to get blown up when assigned to a spare?* His final tasks before leaving the B-25 were making sure all the machine guns were unloaded and secured and the fuel tanks topped off. He turned the B-25 over to the ground crew, then waited for a ride to operations.

Along the northern boundary of the airfield rested derelict German and Italian aircraft, abandoned by the field's previous owners. Those airplanes that were in good shape had long ago been made airworthy and flown to Cairo for evaluation. The remaining examples were little more than carcasses, having been picked over for souvenirs—instruments, lights, controls, wheels. Even the swastika insignias had been cut out, leaving holes in the rudder fins that resembled square-shaped wounds. A breeze batted the ragged remnants of fabric hanging from the airframes. The machines, once the pride of their nation's industry, were now a collection of decrepit junk.

What a waste, mused Bill. Dust carried by the desert wind brushed his face, making him wince, and added to his melancholy funk.

He caught a ride on a parts truck returning to the maintenance hangars. Once there, Bill started toward his tent. Sergeant Dexter was heading the other way, having changed out of his flight overalls and into fatigues. He was tossing a baseball into a fielder's mitt.

"Hey O'Loughlin," Dexter said, "we're organizing a ball game."

Ordinarily, Bill would've claimed a position in the outfield. Baseball was a good way to clear one's head. But not today. "Later maybe."

"Whasamatter?" Dexter asked. "You been acting distracted."

Bill was embarrassed by being so obvious. He hoped he hadn't appeared distracted when handling the 500-pound bombs. "Not feeling well."

"You look fine to me."

"If I give you a cigarette," Bill dug into his breast pocket, "will you leave me alone?"

"What's eatin' you?"

"You want a smoke or not?"

Dexter zipped his lips and held out his fingers. Bill handed him a Lucky Strike.

Bill found his tent deserted. He opened his foot locker and retrieved the object of his distraction, a recent V-Mail letter. He was planning to sit by himself and unravel his thoughts with a cigarette and a cup of coffee. But the tent stove was cold, which meant the coffee pot sitting on top was cold. Lighting the stove was too much trouble and besides, it would take an hour before the stove was hot enough to brew coffee. He stuck the letter in his pocket and headed to the squadron mess hall—formerly a fascist barracks—where the mess sergeant kept fresh donuts and coffee for the returning aircrews.

Bill filled a cup and found a seat in one corner of the mess hall. He reached for the tin can turned ash tray on the center of the table and lit a cigarette.

He pulled the V-Mail envelope from his overalls pocket and removed the letter, carefully unfolding it. He'd devoured the letter when he first received it and reread it to the point that he was surprised that his gaze had not rubbed the words right off the paper. Regulations forbade aircrews from flying with personal mementoes like these letters. The stated reason: should they get shot down, what seemed like innocuous details in the letter could provide the enemy with valuable tidbits of military intelligence.

Inhaling a long drag, the smoke swirled through Bill, calming him like a sedative as he read:

August 24, 1943

Dearest Bill,

Or should I say Daddy? Our baby girl was born yesterday. Just as we decided, I named her Maureen. The name is perfect.

She was born absolutely healthy in every way. When I was holding our little girl, I felt so close to you. It was as if we were all together in that hospital room.

Your sisters Eileen and Marce brought a basket of baby clothes. Now that I'm rested up and able to think clearly, the whole experience is magical and will be even more so when you're with us again.

Wishing you the best. Much love,
Your loving wife, Betty

Bill studied the letter. It was a good facsimile of her hand-writing as the letter was actually a photo of the original.

The letter was a brief missive but it profoundly changed his thinking like the earth itself had been knocked off its axis. In having a baby, he and Betty had brought a new life into being, a new person to carry on the family legacy. He became acutely aware of his place in the world, another thread in the fabric of humanity, now woven to those preceding him and to those who would succeed him. He thought about his father, who died when Bill was a young boy, and so Bill had to fill in the blanks of his expected duties as the man of the house.

But between that and his present circumstances was this war. He fought for hearth and home, and here he was on the other side of the world from both. And like everyone else in uniform, he was in this for the duration, like it or not. There were only three ways to go home. When the war was over, or you got wounded, or were shipped home in a box.

The first option was the only practical choice, however long that took. Wounded? He remembered crippled veterans from the First World War and even old timers from the Civil War, one sleeve or a pants leg pinned up, hobbling around on crutches, defined for the rest of their lives by what was missing. And there was no point in thinking about the third option.

To brighten his thoughts, he reread the letter and tried to imagine seeing Betty as she wrote it. What had she been wearing? How had she fixed her hair? Had she been in bed, propped on pillows? Or was she strong enough to make her way to a table? The letter had been originally completed with an ink pen. Betty took pride in her writing so she probably used her Parker fountain pen. He tried to imagine every step in her process of writing this letter. Selecting the V-Mail stationery, filling the pen with ink, wondering what to write, putting those thoughts to paper, and then handing it over to someone else to post. Who? Eileen? Marce? Florence?

Bill imagined what it would feel like to hold his baby. He caught himself cupping his hands as if Maureen was there resting against his fingers. He had not even seen his daughter and yet missed her so much it hurt.

He stared at the smoke curling from the end of his cigarette. He was no different than those around him, but to each man, the ache of being so far from loved ones pressed down with an enormous and painful gravity.

After one last drag on the Lucky Strike, he slipped the letter back its envelope, then folded the envelope back into his pocket.

October 8, 1943

The Corinthian Sea crawled into view, an expanse of blue streaked with sunlight. Today's mission was a high-altitude attack on a Luftwaffe airfield outside Athens, and Bill flew in aircraft 41-13181, *The Sophisticated Lady.*

He reflected on his world travels, courtesy of Uncle Sam. When he was in school, Africa was a big unknown. But Greece he'd heard about. Heracles, Homer, Achilles, the Spartans, the Athenians, those were names he remembered, though vaguely. He never thought he'd ever visit Greece, let alone that when he did, it would be to rain bombs on who-ever was below. The coastline, rimmed with white limestone gave way to a rugged landscape of dark greens and browns.

"Stay sharp," Captain Beeson the pilot said. "We're over enemy territory and it's gonna be like we kicked a hornet's nest."

From his perch in the tail position, Bill watched the turrets of the trailing bombers rotate, the machine guns panning the heavens. One of the latest modifications had been to enlarge the windows immediately behind the wings and install two machine guns, one firing to port and the other to starboard. This brought the number of defensive guns on each bomber to seven.

"Fighters!" a voice sang out.

Bill's nerves jolted. He craned his neck in every direction in search of the enemy.

"Four bandits. Off to port. Eight o'clock."

Bill pulled against the grips of his machine gun for leverage so he could scoot further into the tail cone for a better view. Sure enough, high and trailing the left rudder of *The Sophisticated Lady*, four dots hovered against the clouds. At any other time, Bill might have dismissed the tiny specks, but now they represented formidable war machines that could close the distance between them and the Mitchells within seconds.

But the enemy aircraft remained in position, their presence taunting the American bombers, reminding them that doom awaited.

Dexter the radioman broke the tension. "What are they waiting for?"

Manning, the turret gunner, answered, "Maybe they heard what good shots we are."

"That ain't it," chimed Davis the bombardier. "They heard about Dexter's ugly mug and came to see for themselves."

"All right," scolded Beeson, "knock off the chatter."

Static and the drone of the engines filled the intercom.

"Messerschmitts!" cried a new voice. "109s! Six o'clock."

Bill strained to count the dots closing the gap behind them and reported, "Two groups of four. Eight fighters total."

Another round of warnings shouted over the intercom. More fighters joined in, now close enough for Bill to recognize their characteristic bullet-shaped propeller spinners and broad tail fins. ME-109s all right.

The fighters separated into two elements of about twelve fighters each. The lead element used their superior speed over the Mitchells to fly ahead while the other element stayed put. Bill recognized the strategy. One group would attack from the front while the other would harry the bombers from behind. The lead element began to spread out.

"It's like they're queueing up for a bread line."

"Here they come!"

Now it starts. Bill swallowed nervously. He took a deep breath and readied himself. *Stay sharp.*

The lead fighter rolled for a wing-over attack and dove for the bombers. The next fighter followed, then the third, and the fourth, peeling after one another, guns ready.

The Messerschmitts focused on the bombers on the left side of the formation. Red tracers sprayed from the B-25s. The fighters tore through the glowing red curtain. Bursts of fire erupted from the noses of the Messerschmitts and white tracers clawed toward the Mitchells.

Rather than break off their attacks, the German pilots raced fearlessly through the American formation, zooming between the bombers like sharks tearing through a school of tuna. *The Sophisticated Lady* shook from the percussion of its machine guns firing in all directions. Tracers crisscrossed the air, weaving a dense pattern of deadly white and red sparks. The fight became a desperate aerial brawl.

A Messerschmitt dashed between *The Sophisticated Lady* and the bomber right behind, the German pilot threading the needle at 350 miles an hour. Bill's mind spun into hyperspeed. He set his gun sights on the fighter and depressed his machine gun's trigger. One instant the enemy was gaining on *The Sophisticated Lady,* then he practically filled the sky with his wings—lizard green over sky blue with black-and-white cross insignia—heedless of the red tracers flinging toward him. Bill glimpsed the pilot's goggled face, then he was gone.

Bill barely had time to catch his breath when another Messerschmitt screamed directly over his aircraft, speeding away, trailing smoke.

"Jesus!" shrieked Manning. "The son of a bitch almost rammed us."

The German fighters climbed and resumed their station just out of reach from the bombers' guns.

Bill wondered why the enemy didn't press another attack. Perhaps they were low on ammo. Or fuel. Regardless, they weren't attacking and that was a good thing. Bill caught his chest heaving from the excitement, and though he hadn't moved much, it felt like he'd sprinted a hundred yards full-speed.

Then Beeson announced, "The fighters are breaking off."

This meant the bombers were entering the flak zone protecting the airfield. Any second now, the sky would be filled with exploding 88s.

The formation flew north of Athens, then circled, angling south for the target. Black bursts of smoke erupted around them, rocking the bombers. Each explosion sounded like the ominous slamming of a door.

Davis relayed the bomb drop instructions. The formation inched closer and the individual aircraft held steady. Bomb bay doors popped open.

Bill recognized the Acropolis far below, a scattering of white ruins, surprisingly visible from ten-thousand feet. But this was good news. If he could see the Acropolis, that meant their bombs would miss. He remembered an admonition from the mission briefing. *The Greeks are our allies. Let's not antagonize them by blowing up their homes and historical treasures.*

On command, each bomber would release a string of six 500-pound bombs, fitted a "quick fuse"—military jargon for immediate detonation. A direct hit on an airplane from this altitude was pure luck. But a bomb exploding within a hundred yards would cause damage but to destroy the aircraft, the bomb had to explode within twenty-five yards. However, bracketing the target would overlap bomb bursts and increase the probability of "useful destruction." The first time Bill heard this term, he thought the explanation sounded remarkably dry, like a dull science lesson, though cold-blooded in its implications.

"Bombs away."

Bombs fell from the B-25s and shrank to disappear in the clutter surrounding the airfield. Clouds of smoke spread into view. Flashes tore through the smoke. Flames licked upward.

Bill noted the damage. "Hits on the hangers." He counted burning dots on the airfield, each representing a destroyed airplane. "Five. Six. Seven airplanes on fire. I'd say forty percent hits on target."

Forty percent on target was actually pretty good shooting, especially against something as spread out as an airfield. Post-mission briefing with photographs would confirm the damage.

The bombers began a shallow, turning dive to gain speed over the Saronic Gulf and escape the anti-aircraft batteries. As expected, once outside the flak zone, the Messerschmitts were waiting, ready to exact revenge.

The aircrew hollered warnings. Red and white tracers clouded the sky. The fighters lashed through the bomber formation. Bill focused on one fighter and led him with a burst from the machine gun. He relaxed only enough to take a deep breath when he heard and felt, a disturbing *th-thump.*

"We've taken a hit," Manning shouted. "Starboard wing."

Bill scooted forward and studied the underside of the right-side wing. Worriedly, he looked for smoke. Thankfully, all he saw was a jagged fist-sized hole. "We're doing okay."

The fighters regrouped and headed north.

"I guess they're calling it a day," Beeson said.

Bill wiped his face and breathed a long sigh of relief. He licked his lips, tasting sweat and gun smoke and oil. The B-25s banked toward the west, crossing the Ionian Sea for the heel of the Italian boot and their new airbase at Grottaglie.

Thoughts about Betty and Maureen crept into his mind. The view out the tail cone of the B-25 was an amazing panorama. It was as if the whole breadth of the world had been laid out for him alone. Someday, he promised himself, he would charter an airplane and bring Betty and Maureen here to retrace his path over the Mediterranean.

After the war.

14

October 21, 1943

After today's mission had been scrubbed on account of rain and fog, Bill and Harold Schrader hitched a ride into Grottaglie, a small down east of the airfield, which the group had recently occupied.

From what Bill understood of the war so far, the Allies had tried a two-prong invasion of Italy. The main landing was at Salerno and the second, smaller landing of British troops at Taranto, an Italian naval base inside the gulf defined by the peninsula's heel. The Taranto attack was a diversion to pin down German forces, away from Salerno and the western coast, where the Allies intended to advance up the peninsula. But the Germans had seen through the ruse and abandoned Taranto after a token defense. That meant that heavy fighting had spared the area but the war still extracted a heavy price from the locals.

He wondered about all the smashed-up local houses and why so many people lived in squalor. Then he learned that

Mussolini was embarrassed by the decrepit state of housing and demolished the old buildings to be replaced by modern structures, the envy of the world the Fascists had promised. Unfortunately, the war interfered with those plans and so those people were left homeless. The average Italian's misery was more the fault of their own government's incompetence than from enemy bombardment.

Bill felt the truck lurch to a halt. He and Schrader slipped out of the cargo bed, water dripping from the canopy onto their heads. Their boots plopped into a dirty puddle. Though the rain had stopped, the air remained dimmed by a cold mist. *So much for sunny Italy.*

Both Bill and Schrader knew there wasn't much to see in town, small as it was, but they were fed up with cabin fever and needed a break from the routine. Now that they were in Grottaglie proper, their low expectations were not disappointed.

Schrader gazed up and down the streets feeding the intersection, a jumble of old stucco and brick buildings that sagged against one another. The doors and windows were shut tight against the cold, and the effect made them feel unwelcome.

"So what now?" Schrader flipped up his coat collar to ward off the chill. He began to regret leaving his tent and its ready supply of hot coffee.

Bill pointed. "That way."

After a few steps, Bill heard laughter. Up ahead, an American GI exited the doorway of a two-story building, the laugher spilling past a canvas tarp blocking the entrance. A couple of Jeeps and a Dodge staff car were parked in front, along the edge of the rain-spattered road.

"The place looks popular," Bill said enthusiastically. "I'll bet they got something that'll wet my whistle."

They jogged across the muddy street and slipped past the tarp to enter a makeshift saloon. GIs stood in clusters scattered about the room, their laughter and exclamations overlapping into a loud mumble. Because of the damp uniforms, the place smelled like a kennel of wet dogs. A layer of cigarette smoke shimmered just over their heads, the smoke illuminated by electric ceiling lights. Electricity meant, considering the dilapidated state of affairs in the rest of the town, that whoever ran this establishment had pull with the authorities.

Bill and Schrader moved warily toward the bar, actually a door propped on wine casks. Considering that they were among fellow Americans they should've felt at ease. But the truth was that not all was harmonious with the GIs. The ground troops expressed envy at those from the Army Air Force, claiming they were pampered momma's boys. The belief was that aircrews buzzed over the torn up Italian landscape while the ground troops had to slog through the mud. And the aircrews returned to dry cots kept cozy warm by friendly nurses.

Actually, the infantry and the others who did the hard fighting weren't at all envious. They appreciated when the air force arrived to bomb and strafe the enemy. And they'd witness first-hand when an airplane was blown out of the sky and crash as a flaming wreck.

It was the rear-echelon soldiers who were the trouble makers, having too much free time on their hands. Collectively they were known as "garri-troopers." *Too far forward to wear neckties, too far back to get shot at.*

Bill and Schrader found a gap along the crowded bar. The bartender had a narrow face and sported a recent haircut. He wore GI-issue clothing: olive-drab trousers, boots, khaki shirt sans tie, the sleeves rolled up. With deft movements, he poured booze into a line of glasses. He acknowledged Bill and Schrader with a nod and then spoke around the cigarette in his mouth. "Whaddya guys have?" His accent was very American.

"This your place?" Bill asked.

"I'm partners." The bartender tipped his head to an older Italian man at a corner table, flanked by two young women. In a stairway along the back wall, another GI, one with a satisfied grin on his face, clomped down the steps as he tucked his shirt into his trousers. Bill gazed up at the ceiling and imagined what was happening on the second floor. *Drinks weren't the only thing this place was selling.*

Schrader leaned over the bar to examine the bottles on a back shelf. "You got Old Crow whiskey?"

"If you see it, I got it."

"Is it legit?"

The bar tender knit his brow. "You callin' me a cheat?"

Schrader reached into a coat pocket. "I'll take my chances. How much?"

"A dollar."

"A buck for a shot of booze?"

"The door's behind you, mack."

Bill nudged Schrader to calm him. Bill asked, "How much for grappa?"

"A quarter a glass."

Bill sighed in disbelief. This guy was gouging them. But they'd come into town for some diversion and other than going upstairs—which wasn't going to happen—and risking the clap or crabs, they'd have to make do with a drink.

He laid a couple of quarters on the counter. The bartender plunked down two glasses and poured into each, three fingers of grappa.

Bill examined his drink. "At least the glasses look clean."

He'd never heard of grappa before arriving in Italy. He learned it was made from the skins and stems leftover from the mashing of wine grapes. Supposedly, good grappa made for an acceptable cordial, but fat chance that as GIs that they'd find anything but the cheap stuff.

Schrader held his glass "The trick to enjoying grappa is to avoid getting a whiff of it. The smell will sting your eyes."

This Bill already knew. He and Schrader clinked glasses and each gulped a swallow. The burning sensation was every bit as unpleasant as the last time he'd guzzled the stuff.

Bill blew air out his mouth to cool his tongue. The alcohol blasted right through him, bringing its reward, a ninety-proof kick.

Another swallow waited in the glass. Though Bill had had enough, he'd paid for the grappa and so emptied the glass. The harshness bit, then ebbed, replaced by a pleasant buzz.

He offered a smoke to Schrader and took one for himself.

The bartender returned. "Another round?"

Bill shook his head. One glass was enough. Any more and a headache would plague him the next day. Plus, he was scheduled for a mission tomorrow and the last thing he needed was to handle bombs while hungover. He and Schrader stood side by side, puffing on cigarettes, content to be here, pretending that the war was far away. His thoughts drifted to Chicago. And Betty. Maureen. What he wouldn't give to be back with them. Be done with this crummy war.

He lit another smoke and let the nicotine buzz braid with the lingering effects of the grappa. It was too easy to spiral down black thoughts. That didn't get you anywhere. Complaining about it with your buddies didn't get far either because they'd tell you to suck it up. Everyone had their private worries.

Though content with one glass of grappa, Bill wasn't ready to leave. And go where? Back to the airfield? Curfew was six o'clock, which meant be home before dark. Sound advice really, as stumbling though these streets invited attention from criminals.

Halfway through the second cigarette someone bumped him rudely from the side. Startled, he turned his head, expecting an apology.

Instead, a short GI with a greasy mop of hair glared at him. "Hey fellas, look who's here! One of them fly boys. Must be nice, taking a break from the war on account of rain."

What gave Bill away was his shoulder patch of the Fifteen Air Force. The other guy wore a patch of the Fifth Army, which meant this little weasel was assigned to a headquarters unit, not a combat outfit. Garri-trooper for sure.

Bill raised his hands. "I don't want trouble." In the last year he'd yo-yoed from sergeant to tech/sergeant and back and didn't want to risk a stripe on account of this fool.

"Course you don't want trouble," the garri-trooper sneered. "That's why you joined the air corps. If there's a war to fight, can't be a cushier place than up there." He twirled a finger toward the ceiling.

Bill turned away from him.

The garri-trooper grabbed Bill's arm. "I'm talking to you."

The goodwill inside Bill poured right out of him, replaced by a sourness like he was eating raw cabbage. A wall of soldiers crowded close. The air became brittle with tension.

The bartender slapped the counter. "You guys wanna rumble, take it outside." He looked at his Italian partner. "Another fight breaks out, the MPs will shut us down. We'll be placed off-limits."

Bill pulled his arm free of the garri-trooper's grasp. The garri-trooper smirked. "Too yellow to fight?"

"That's not it. It's that your problems are not my problems."

"Oh yeah," replied the garri-trooper. "And what might those problems be other than I'm standing next to a coward?"

Bill studied the gazes measuring him. No way was he going to allow this midget the last word. "Your problem is that you're not just short but ugly."

In the wavering light of the electric bulbs, the garri-trooper's complexion reddened several shades. Bill knew what was next. Before the little loud mouth could throw a punch, Bill shoved him backwards. That ignited a brawl and a volley of fists came at him from all directions. A blow landed on Bill's cheek, knocking him against the bar. A hand grabbed his shoulder and yanked him across the floor. Bill scrambled to gain his balance but the hand kept hauling him through the swirl of bodies. He found himself stumbling outside, Schrader pulling him along.

"Damn you, O'Loughlin," Schrader exclaimed, "did you have to razz that guy?"

Bill rubbed his face where it smarted from the blow. He examined his empty fingers.

"What's wrong?" Schrader asked.

"I lost my cigarette."

Schrader laughed and pushed him down the street. "C'mon, let's get back before curfew."

Bill checked his watch. They had a couple of hours to walk the two miles though a ride would be nice.

The rumble of a Jeep approached from behind. Both Bill and Schrader turned around, hoping to thumb a lift. But as soon as he saw the headgear of the driver and his front seat passenger, he decided against. They were French troops, recognizable by their distinctive caps. The campaign against the Germans was supposed to be an Allied effort, but the French acted as if they were doing everyone else a favor by participating in the war. They drove American jeeps and trucks, wore American uniforms and field gear, fired American guns, yet they proved to be the stingiest of all. They'd offer a ride, for a price like they were taxis.

Well, *screw these frogs.* Bill and Schrader put their backs to them. The Jeep bounced by, splashing mud, the passengers not even acknowledging these American allies.

Once back at the airfield, after dinner and a pre-mission briefing, Bill joined his buddies back at the tent. The time was a little after eight but they were already snug in their cots. Tomorrow's wakeup was 4 a.m. The squadron would take off at 7:10 a.m. In between those times, Bill had to eat breakfast, attend the mission briefing, make sure his assigned aircraft was ready, and supervise the loading of the bombs.

A gas lantern hissed from where it hung on a tent pole. Bill stared at a blank V-Mail and pondered what to write Betty. He had much to relate but little opportunity to do so. The censors combed through every letter and marked out any offending details with stripes of black ink so Bill had to be careful in what he mentioned. Plus, the V-Mail letter didn't offer much space to write. A few paragraphs at most. Brief ones at that.

One bit of news that they'd received was that the airfield would be deploying forward. Where to? For now, that was a secret. The group hadn't yet been at Grottaglie a month yet and already they were advancing up the peninsula?

What amazed Bill the most about the American way of war was the US's ability to move mountains of men and equipment across oceans and continents. He imagined combat as a chessboard, individual pieces moving in strategic maneuvers but the US could bend the rules by piling pieces in front of an enemy so that the battle was decided by sheer force of numbers. What had he heard in history class? That Napoleon said, *God is on the side of the big battalions.*

Quantity was helpful but Bill had seen enough to know that it was up to individuals doing their little part that allowed the larger whole to prevail. Each bomb that hit its target had done so because every man on the B-25 had applied himself to the task. They flew straight into the enemy's teeth and coolly delivered the goods, in their case, 500-pound bombs and buckets of .50 caliber ammunition. Mission by mission, bomb by bomb, dead German by dead German, the 321st Bombardment Group was tilting the odds toward an Allied victory.

When at the briefing, Bill had spent several minutes studying a map of the theater of operations—North Africa, the Mediterranean, Sicily, Italy, Greece, the Balkans, southern France. In less than a year, the Americans and their allies had punched their way over the Mediterranean and gained ground on southern Italy. The progress so far had been remarkable. Looking at it with hindsight, he could almost convince himself that the advances were inevitable. But the British had been fighting since 1940, sacrificing tens of thousands. Though the Germans had also suffered considerable losses, their tenacity increased the farther they withdrew into the European continent. There was still a lot of bitter combat ahead.

Bill had to sort through his mind what to write. Besides the fighting itself, he wanted to write about his experiences overseas. He thought about venting his spleen about the

French. But that might be a no-no to the censors. Among the Allies, it was supposed to be all harmony.

The enlisted men groused about the preferential treatment the officers allowed themselves. They were first in line to pilfer captured stores of liquor. You'd never see a colonel or general drink cut-rate grappa, only the best bottles. The American high command saw no irony in the fact that the plush offices they moved into were recently vacated by the fascist high command. One set of pompous asses replaced another. Bill chuckled at the thought. Definitely couldn't mention that.

He decided what to write and readied his pen, dating the letter for tomorrow and adding clues about where he was.

October 22, 1943

Sweetheart,

Another day in a not-so-sunny area on the other side of the world. The rain reminds me of Chicago, which in turn reminds me of you and the spaghetti parlor down the street. The people here are grateful for our presence and American dollars. And whatever they can steal, which they are good at.

How is everyone at home? Mom? Marce? Tell Eileen to send more cookies.

We have plenty of coffee and hot donuts to keep us warm. Our airplanes are good mounts, like the faithful horses in a cowboy movie. Everyone is in fine spirits considering we're so far from home and our loved ones.

When you have the chance, please send a photo of our little girl. A minute doesn't go by that I don't think of her and you. Regards to everyone at home. I'll see you soon, God willing.

All my love, darling,

Bill

15

January 10, 1944

D ear Princess:

I received a letter from Bob today and one from Eileen a couple of days ago, which were written early in December but I haven't had any from you for quite a while now, darling.

The mail hasn't been coming through lately so one of these days I'll get a fistful of letters from you, I hope. The letter from Eileen explained that operation business. I was rather worried at first until I found out what it was all about. Having an operation on her eye seems to indicate she is dead serious about joining the "Women's Marine Corps."

If I was home, I'd put her over my knee but unfortunately, I'm not home and my letter, ever if it would stop her, will get there too late. This lack of mail also has me worrying about Marce. I certainly hope I get some news soon. How are you and Maureen getting along, hon? I hope all the colds and such are over with for good. You know, sweetheart, it's hard to believe the *baby is almost five months old. At this rate she will be walking before I get to see her.*

No matter how I try to keep it out of my mind, I can't help dreaming of the time when I'll see her in person and I can take both of you into my arms, princess.

Love, Bill.

January 11, 1944

The drone of approaching aircraft filled the air. Like everyone else in the group, Bill hopped a ride to the airfield to welcome the bombers. He hadn't flown a mission since last Saturday, the fateful day when the 447th lost the *Lumber Wagon*.

From this distance, the Mitchells resembled a flock of pigeons jockeying for landing position. The formation stretched into a long queue and one by one, the B-25s touched down and taxied toward parking. News from the tower was that no aircraft had been shot down. Even knowing that, Bill found himself counting the bombers returning to the roost.

In this case, the roost was the airfield just outside Amendola, near Foggia, about fifteen miles from the eastern coast with the Adriatic Sea. The group had deployed here last November, moving north from Grottaglie as part of the big push to keep pressure on the retreating Germans.

Though the ambulances—the "meat wagons"—were on standby, none were needed. Good. That meant no wounded aboard.

After confirming that all the aircraft and crew were back safe, Bill hitched a ride to Group Operations for the post-mission critique.

Group Operations was inside a stone building, formerly the estate stable. The better horses had since been confiscated by the fascists while those too old or lame for military work were stolen, carved up, and eaten by the locals.

Captain Haven, the group's intelligence officer, climbed on the wooden dais along the back of the room and began the briefing. He had broad cheeks and sandy hair. In his New England accent, he addressed the men crowded into the rows of folding chairs. "Let me tell you what we know about our plane from the 448th that was shot down last Friday. Out of the crew of seven, we lost one, KIA, the bombardier, Lieutenant Marvin Matkins."

A groan rippled through the crowd.

"But there is good news." Haven allowed for a dramatic pause. "The other six survived, at first taken POW, then liberated by partisans, and now returned to friendly lines."

Cheers thundered in the room.

Haven rapped his pointer against one of the briefing boards to silence the room. "Now an update on the *Lumber Wagon*." He put the end of the pointer over a map of the Adriatic Sea. "P-40s and Spitfires conducted a sweep where the *Lumber Wagon* went down."

While Bill appreciated the extraordinary lengths the Army Air Force would take to recover or at least eliminate all doubt about the fate of a lost aircrew, he knew that *Lumber Wagon's* situation was hopeless. Since the bomber belonged to the 447th, Bill had known every crewman personally. The pilot, 1LT Graham. The co-pilot, 1LT Briskey. The bombardier, 1LT Kingsley. The radioman, SSGT Mays. The turret gunner, SGT Reilly. And the flight engineer, Cpl Jeffery.

The mission had been a strike across the Adriatic into Yugoslavia, where they bombed German-held marshalling yards at Metkovic. The bombs had patterned in near textbook fashion, cratering railroad tracks and roads, and blasting the warehouses, leaving them in flames. Flak had been heavy, but inaccurate.

However, during the bomb run, four FW-190s braved their own anti-aircraft fire and lunged after the Mitchells, diving through the formation in head-on attacks. When the bombers turned from the target toward Italy, a second, larger group of German fighters, ME-109s, joined the fray. The Luftwaffe pilots showed their experience, lashing at the B-25s in bold, calculating attacks either from the front, or from behind. Bill had managed several bursts against the enemy.

Three enemy fighters had been shot down but that was little comfort against the sight of the *Lumber Wagon* as it limped out of formation, its port engine on fire. Every man aloft in the 447th watched and prayed for a miracle. But once outside the defensive fire of their fellow bombers, Lieutenant Graham and his men were on their own against the swarm of fighters.

Bill remembered watching the B-25 shrink into the distance until it was a spot in the air trailing a feather of smoke. He had imagined the desperation of the crew, Graham and Briskey wrestling with the controls, while the gunners fought back with their machine guns even as the barrels glowed red hot. The interior deck was certainly ankle-deep in spent .50 caliber cartridge casings and belt links, the air thick with smoke from the over-worked guns and the burning airplane.

Minute-by-minute, the German pilots closed the trap, raking the Mitchell with bullets and 20mm cannon shells, punishing man and machine with equal fury. The final moments aboard the bomber must've been absolute hell, the crew valiantly fighting back with blood-stained hands.

Lumber Wagon struggled to reach the Italian countryside when it at last plunged into the sea, disintegrating on impact. No one witnessed any parachutes.

Six good men. Dead.

Someone tapped Bill's shoulder. Bill jumped, becoming aware again of where he was.

"You all right?" It was Harold Dexter.

"I'm fine," Bill replied.

Dexter offered a pack of smokes. Bill shook one out. Dexter gestured for him to pass the pack down the row.

Bill inhaled the cigarette smoke and let it flow into him, a warm comforting embrace from within. His thoughts settled and he was able to turn his attention back to Captain Haven, who shuffled across the dais to another map as he gathered details from the aircrews about today's mission.

Target, the railroad junction at Falconara. Twenty-three bombers had taken off, one turned back because of an oil leak. The group had flown northeast over the Adriatic, then crossed the coast over the port town of Ancona, proceeding directly to Falconara. Cloud cover had been 4/10 stratocumulus at 6,000 feet, 15 miles visibility, slight haze.

At 1330 hours, on an axis of attack of 160 degrees, from altitudes between 10,500 and 11,000 feet, the formation of 22 bombers had dropped 71, 500-pound bombs, fuses set at 0.1 seconds or .025 seconds delay.

The bombs strung along the target, demolishing the tracks and the rail station, hitting the docks and several barracks, setting them on fire.

Very light flak, inaccurate. No enemy fighters. Thankfully.

The briefing concluded, Captain Haven slapped the pointer across the palm of one hand and rocked on his heels. "Overall," he declared, "a successful mission. And as a bonus, everyone came back in one piece."

The day ended with dinner and an early return to their tents and cots. Bill wondered what to write to Betty. The *Lumber Wagon* was the second bomber lost since the new year began. Their flight engineer was an especially young kid, a corporal no less, James Jeffery, though Bill knew him simply as Jimmy. It didn't seem right for someone with so much life ahead of him to get killed like this. Why stop there? What was right about any aboard the *Lumber Wagon* dying? Or anyone else in the 321st Bombardment Group?

Both the chaplain and the flight surgeon advised the flight crews to talk out their anxieties but to not dwell on them. Don't be a Pollyanna but don't get into such a funk that your misery becomes a self-fulfilling prophesy. Remember, *this too, shall pass.*

Bill decided to ponder the bigger picture. Last October, the Italians threw in the towel and asked for an armistice. The hope was that Italians would switch sides and help fight the Germans. Which sort of happened. The Italians in the south embraced the Allies while to the north, the Italians remained staunchly fascist and eager to fight alongside the Nazis.

The scuttlebutt passed among the American soldiers was: "We got all the loser Italians, the thieves and diseased whores while the Krauts got the Italians with the guts and the brains."

Like all good jokes, it was grounded in truth. Despite the high-minded talk about a united front of Italians fighting shoulder-to-shoulder with the Allies, it seemed as though the Americans were instead saddled with administering a populace on the brink of starvation who showed their gratitude by stealing everything left unguarded.

So much to say. But what to write in his next letter home? Bill sipped from his coffee and inhaled another long drag from his Lucky Strike.

Wednesday, January 12, 1944

What heralded a change from the usual mission were the type of bombs delivered to the flight line. Standard ordnance was 500 pounders. This morning, each bomber was loaded with three 1000 pounders. Whatever the target, it was in for a beating.

After Bill readied his aircraft, 41-12310 *Buckeye Cannon Ball*, he returned to group operations for the mission briefing. When there, he picked up an unexpected buzz from the planning staff. Rumor filtered that a new "high-priority" mission had been just assigned to the 321st, which, combined with the change of bomb loads, added to the mystery of today's target.

Captain Haven and a gaggle of assistants were hastily pinning maps and diagrams to the briefing boards.

First roll call, then the room was turned over to the captain. He gestured with his pointer. "As background for today's mission, the Germans have established the Gustav Line north of Naples. It's a line of formidable defenses—trenchworks, pill boxes, mine fields—centered on Mount Cassino and stretch across the Liri Valley to overlook the Rapido and Garigiliano Rivers." Haven indicated the area.

"You guys know how mountainous the terrain is. The rough slopes channel tanks and trucks into the valleys which the enemy has mined and sighted for artillery. Our infantry has to pry the Germans from the surrounding hills. And if the fighting isn't miserable enough, this Italian winter has been especially fierce and bitter cold."

Haven paced to the next map. "What the Germans have done is flood the rivers, turning the basins into swamps. For our tanks to move, they have to get up on higher ground, on the main roads basically, where the Germans can pick them off with anti-tank guns and artillery. The infantry and other supporting troops don't have an easier time of it either."

The captain turned his attention to a large diagram. "This is today's target, the Isoletta Dam. It's from here that the Germans are manipulating the flood gates to control the waters flowing into the rivers. They aim to turn the river basins into quagmires. As long as they can do that, our ground forces can't" —Haven swept his pointer north—"break out and advance north to Rome. Busting the Isoletta Dam is key to the whole show."

Haven sidestepped to the next briefing board, one with a large black and white photo of the dam, obviously taken by a reconnaissance aircraft. The reservoir itself was a series of oblong bodies of water that narrowed to the dam. Not only was the dam small, not even a hundred yards wide, it was fronted downstream by a concrete bridge that served as a shield.

"Your aircraft have been loaded with thousand pounders and you'll need to score several direct hits to break the dam."

Someone shouted, "What if we just damage the damn dam?"

Laughter from the aircrews.

Haven nodded as he mulled the question. "I guess if the Germans can't operate the floodgates, that might help. But it's better to knock the dam out once and for all."

Mumbled comments circulated about the room.

Bill scrutinized the photo of the dam and the situation map of the ground battle. The Isoletta Dam was about eighteen miles northwest of Cassino. He could see how demolishing the dam would affect the offensive. Break the dam, and *voila!* the tanks and infantry would charge to Rome. At least, that's the way the history books would write it down. But from his perch as tail gunner on a B-25, he knew that both on the ground and in the air, the fight up the Italian boot was a long, desperate battle.

Haven banged his pointer on a briefing stand to gain attention. "Since we know how important the Isoletta Dam is, the Krauts know it as well." Haven drew a circle with his pointer around the dam. "They've recently emplaced batteries of 88mm and 105mm flak guns to protect it from air attack."

Several of the men whistled in bemused amazement.

Haven continued. "The 88s are deadly enough, but the 105s have a longer reach, fire a larger shell, and are in this case, manned by elite, seasoned gunners."

He replaced the photo of the dam with a similar-sized photo montage of radar antennae. "To make matters more troubling, the Germans are covering the dam with radar, both early-warning and targeting."

Bill let this fact sink in. Early warning radar eliminated the element of surprise, always something to have on your side. The presence of targeting radar was especially ominous. Typically, flak guns were fired to barrage a box in the sky and hopefully hit any aircraft bracketed within the box. Targeting radar meant the defenders would select an individual aircraft and direct the guns against it.

"The 321st won't be striking the dam alone. Spitfires and P-38s will provide top cover against German fighters. A-36s and P-40s will dive bomb and strafe the anti-aircraft positions, clearing the way for you guys." Haven offered a tight grin that Bill interpreted as *hopefully*.

In the year since the Army Air Force had fought its way across North Africa, then the Mediterranean, now Italy, the

German flak gunners had gained plenty of target practice. Hardly a mission passed without at least several aircraft from the 15th Air Force getting shot out of the sky. Add mishaps caused by the mercurial weather, and the odds got stacked against you.

Captain Haven quit brandishing the pointer. "This concludes the intelligence portion of the briefing. Major Taylor from Group Operations will fill you in on the mission details. As of now, take-off time is 1245 hours so plan accordingly." Haven cleared his throat. "Good luck."

16

Wednesday, January 12, 1944

When the pilot, Lt. Frederick Vincent, gave the okay, Bill unfolded himself from his seat behind the cockpit and stood, anchoring himself against Vincent's seatback. The *Buckeye Cannon Ball* swayed around him. He scoped out the engine gauges on the instrument panel. The takeoff had been worrisome because the port engine didn't have time for a proper warmup. Only minutes ago it finally reached operational temperature.

Bill keyed his intercom. "How's the engine looking?"

The co-pilot, 1st Lt. John Haeberle, tapped the engine gauges in turn, oil temperature and cylinder head temperature. Without looking away, he gave the thumbs up. "Running smooth, O'Loughlin."

Satisfied that the airplane wouldn't drop out of the mission, Bill turned his attention out the windshield. Eighteen aircraft had departed for the attack and, at the moment, his airplane was in the middle of the queue, a ragged line climbing slowly into the heavens.

After several minutes, the bombers reached cruising altitude and assembled into combat formation. The 445th and 446th Squadrons formed into the first flight. The 447th and 448th Squadrons made the second flight. The *Buckeye Cannon Ball* slid to the right of the squadron's lead aircraft, *Shad Rack You Done Crapped Again*, piloted by 1st Lieutenant Thomas.

Cruising at six thousand feet, the Mitchells flew through wisps of stratocumulus clouds. The aircraft banked, turning to the next heading, 249 degrees, flying southwest, which meant they were over Lucera, the first checkpoint. Lieutenant Vincent gave the order for everyone to take their gunnery stations. Bill unplugged his headset and made his way to the rear of the fuselage. S.Sgt. Harold Schrader was already crawling into his turret basket. The radioman S.Sgt. Donald Davis stood beside the port waist window and fed a belt of ammo into that gun. Sgt. Leo Hassett was busy loading the starboard waist gun. The *Buckeye Cannon Ball* was the squadron's designated bomber to photograph the attack, and so Hassett was onboard to operate the camera fitted in the aircraft's belly.

Winter temperature on the ground had been comfortable enough but now at altitude, Bill appreciated his bulky insulated overalls and fleece-lined leather jacket. When he reached the rear of the fuselage, he shucked his parachute, stowed it, dropped to his knees, and crawled into the tail cone. He tugged a belt of machine gun cartridges from the ammo box and fed it into the gun's receiver, then plugged into the intercom, hearing Lieutenant Vincent say, "Whenever you're ready, test fire your guns."

The staccato blasts of the bomber's machine guns reverberated throughout the fuselage.

"Nose guns, okay." That was S.Sgt. Wille Franklin, the bombardier.

Davis: "Port gun, ready."

Hassett: "Starboard gun, okay."

Schrader: "Turret guns, okay."

Bill yanked the charging handle of his gun and selected a clear spot in the air to fire into. The spade grips shook in his hands and the machine gun's muzzle spat a line of red tracers that arced into the distance. "Tail gun, ready."

All around him, muzzle flashes and dots of tracers sprayed from the other bombers. He rolled back his jacket cuff to read the time. 3:10 p.m. Another fifty minutes to target. Now wait. Observe.

High above, the sun glowed through altostratus unraveling like loose yarn against the azure expanse. The light was bright enough for Bill to lower his tinted lenses over his goggles.

Previous missions had proceeded north over the Adriatic Sea so it was fascinating to fly right over the mountainous spine of the Italian peninsula. Snow draped the rugged mountains, gray and beige. The valleys were muddy brown basins spread around rivers coiling between the hills.

Low white clouds drifted into view. He couldn't tell if it was smoke or midday fog. Maybe it was a fierce ground battle. Artillery? Tanks going at it? He'd heard stories that in the mountain fighting, at the far end of the logistical tail, that the combatants sometimes ran out of ammunition and threw rocks at each other. It conjured such a bizarre image that he hoped it was true.

He burped. Prior to the mission, they had been fed ham and cheese sandwiches. They were due over the target at 1400 hours to return to the airfield by 1530. The schedule was so routine that it was practically banker's hours.

The habitual drill could lull one into complacency. About every ten minutes, Lieutenant Vincent keyed the intercom for an update to make sure everyone was awake and paying attention.

For Bill that wasn't a problem. Witnessing the loss of the *Lumber Wagon* had made him keenly aware that the end could come at any time. Considering the growing ferocity of the German defenses, it wasn't a surprise that they'd take down one of the bombers. But on any given mission, which unlucky airplane would draw the short straw? It happened so randomly. To ward off bad luck, a lot of the guys kept lucky talismans, or indulged in rituals, or got extra religious.

Everyone was cognizant of their mortality and what they had to lose.

Many of the men had gotten married seemingly at the last minute like Bill had done. During odd moments, they wondered out loud if it was worth it, burdening yourself with concerns of who would be left behind should the worst happen. In those situations, keeping yourself alive was no longer just about you but about what you owed your wife and maybe kids as well. Too many were like Bill, a newlywed wife back home, with a kid that may not ever see their father.

The *Buckeye Cannon Ball* banked to the right. They had reached another checkpoint. The closer the group flew toward the target, the more the formation tightened. The terrain below was a confused jumble of mountains and hills and narrow valleys. Looking to starboard, he noted a white clutter of buildings atop a prominent mountain. That had to be Cassino. Which meant they were deep over enemy territory.

The formation made a new turn and began to climb: the second checkpoint. Bill took the opportunity to check out the aircraft behind his. So far, so good.

He'd been thinking about being a father who had yet to see his daughter. But that pessimistic view of matters was offset by the memories of time with Betty where every moment had been more precious than diamonds. Against a screen in his mind's eye, Bill could project every minute they had spent together in North Carolina when she had arrived to marry him. He remembered Joe Parisi's expression when he saw that Bill had worn his shoes to the wedding.

Hassett broke the silence. "Camera's ready."

The bombers turned again. Bill noted they were at attack altitude, ten thousand feet.

The previous thoughts resumed, flitting back and forth through his head. At this height above Italy, on the hard edge between two powerful nations locked in bitter combat, he perceived himself as a sharp gear in a powerful and dangerous machine. It didn't dismay him or depersonalize him. On the contrary, it made him more appreciative of his important part in this crusade to annihilate the Nazis.

He let the grandiose notion simmer a bit before passing it out of his mind. He turned his attention to the bomber trailing his, aircraft 695. For some reason, that aircraft hadn't been given a name. The flight engineer was S. Sgt. Delore Monroe. A decent enough fellow. Hell, everybody in the group was a decent enough fellow.

Bill recalled the long path here. Basic training. The days in Inglewood. Flights over the California deserts and coastline. Crew training in North Carolina. The jump to Florida, then Belize, Brazil, across the Atlantic to the Ascension Islands, arriving in the Gold Coast of Africa. Then deployment north to begin combat operations against the Germans and Italians.

The formation made a sharp turn to the right. Ten minutes to the target. Bill clenched his jaw and pulled closer to his machine gun. Looking down, the Sacco River Valley snaked across the hilly landscape as it fed into the Isoletta Dam reservoir. A reflection of the sun raced along the twisting river, the spot of light disappearing at the sharp bends, then appearing again.

Explosions barked in the distance. Fear plucked Bill's nerves. He glanced in the direction of the noise and caught sight of the ugly black puffs of smoke marking where the flak shells had exploded.

Lieutenant Vincent said, "The Jerries have rolled out their welcome mat."

More explosions blasted around them. The bombers juked and bucked to throw off the enemy's aim.

Previous targets had been railroad marshalling yards, enemy supply dumps and bivouacs, targets that spread across acres. The group would release its bombs as one, knowing they'd rain steel and high explosive across the target area.

But the Isoletta Dam was a different situation. Each squadron would wait its turn at bat. Six aircraft dropping a total of eighteen, 1000 pounders. Surely, they'd get enough hits to demolish the dam. This was why the 321st was selected. You needed a knockout punch delivered, they were the best.

The bombers turned right again. "Okay boys," Lieutenant Vincent said, "we're over the IP." The bombers eased closer to assure a tight pattern of bombs on a northwest to southeast axis across the face of the dam.

Flak bunched around the formation, the explosions slamming the aircraft. Bill heard and felt a *ping*, like a rock striking the fender of a car.

"We took a hit," Davis exclaimed.

"Jesus Christ!" exclaimed Schrader. "This flak is thick enough to walk on!"

The aircraft of the flight opened their bomb bay doors.

Franklin said, "Bombs ready to drop."

Flak shells detonated around them, getting closer with each passing second. Black clouds burst all around, the explosions overlapping one another into a continuous roar.

Another volley of explosions bracketed the *Buckeye Cannon Ball.*

Another *ping!*

"Bombs away," Franklin announced.

Great, thought Bill, let's get the hell out of here. He scooted right up against his machine gun for a better view of the target.

The fat 1000 pounders sank toward the earth. Falling. Falling. Falling. Now barely dots.

The narrow finger of the reservoir that fed against the dam came into view. Then the dam itself, a curl of pale concrete, which, though small at this altitude, still looked impressive. He caught sight of the bridge just south of the dam.

Explosions walked across the settlement west of the dam. Several white circles blossomed in the water. A bomb struck the bridge. Flak bursts slammed the *Buckeye Cannon Ball*. A veil of dust and smoke drew across the dam, obscuring any damage.

Bill felt a rush that bound all the aircraft together. A sense of relief that with the bombs let loose, the mission was on its downward slope and all they needed to do was ride out the clock and get home safe.

But the Germans didn't let up. The evil black clouds of exploding 88 and 105mm shells followed the bomber.

Franklin yelled over the intercom, "Strafe those bastards!" Then . . .

The *Buckeye Cannon Ball* jolted as if kicked. Bill slammed against the metal bracing of the tail cone. Static blasted through the intercom. A huge flame lashed the starboard side of the fuselage.

Terror stabbed into Bill, causing a panic that filled him with doom. His mouth turned instantly dry and metallic.

The starboard rudder ripped free, followed by the wing twisting loose, and the *Buckeye Cannon Ball* rolling to starboard. Seen through the tail cone canopy, ground became sky. The rolling motion caused Bill's guts to slosh inside his belly.

He clutched the sides of the tail cone to steady himself even as his mind scrambled for a way out. He glimpsed the other bombers, pulling away. Then one, two, three bodies tumbled past. Who had escaped? A parachute billowed open. In that fleeting moment, Bill wished he could trade places.

The broken airplane bucked and kept rolling, the violent motions pinning Bill in place. His terror kicked up when he smelled gas, meaning the fuel lines had been ripped open. The gale force wind funneled the spray of fuel throughout the gyrating bomber.

The *Buckeye Cannon Ball* spun downwards, the centrifugal force pressing Bill against one side of the tail cone. His world devolved into a kaleidoscope of sensations that smeared into each other.

He kicked and tried to pry himself loose. His mind screamed. *Get out. Get the parachute.* But under the best conditions he'd have to shimmy out and try as he might, that was now impossible.

The airplane continued to spin, pressing him against the inside of the fuselage.

Then he found himself weightless, bouncing inside the tail position, smacking against the grips of the machine gun. The belt of cartridges had been knocked loose and whipped around him.

The world outside the tail cone was bright yellow and ribboned with black smoke. He was able to glance between his flailing legs, past his boots, toward his parachute.

The fuselage trembled and kept whirling and whirling.

Unable to comprehend the disaster, all Bill could do was clench his eyes. His brain sensed the inevitable doom and shut down.

Everyone to the rear of the wing remained trapped: Bill, Schrader the turret gunner, Hassett the photographer, and Davis the radioman. The *Buckeye Cannon Ball* fell from the sky a flaming wreck and crashed into the side of a mountain.

None still aboard the aircraft survived.

17

February 1, 1944

Betty had just changed Maureen's diaper when a knock sounded on the front door. She was not expecting anyone and glanced at the clock. The time was 11:42.

She lowered Maureen into the crib and tucked her under a blanket. The knocking repeated. "Coming," Betty said as she stepped to the door. Before reaching for the doorknob she paused to check herself in the small mirror by the door and tap her curls into place.

Out of habit, she fixed a smile and opened the door. At that instant, the blue of the Western Union uniform bloomed before her eyes.

An icy fear lay its hand on the back of Betty's neck. The breath clogged in her throat even as her chest felt like it was collapsing. A tremble wiggled down the base of her skull, down her spine to her arms and legs to tingle her fingers and toes.

The messenger was not a teenager, but an older man, forties maybe with a ruddy complexion pinched red by the

214 | MARK VERWIEL

winter chill. Gray eyes glimmered from within slits in his doughy face. "Mrs. Betty O'Loughlin?"

Her smile remained frozen and all she could manage as a slight nod.

"Telegram." He offered a white envelope.

Her gaze dropped to the envelope. She didn't want to take it, thinking that if she refused, then whatever bad news it had surely brought could not have happened.

For the first time in her life she heard her pulse, a hammering in her ears. As she reached for the envelope, the hammering grew louder, deafening.

The next moments decoupled as if time had fallen apart. The messenger was walking from her, then she was on the sofa, then the messenger was still at the door, she was pacing to the sofa, she was closing the door.

Then time reassembled itself and she was midway toward the sofa. Her thoughts clutched for hope but it was like she was swatting at ribbons of smoke. She wanted to convince herself that the telegram might be good news. Something other than what she knew was inevitable.

Try as she might, she couldn't ignore the reality of the evidence. The smooth texture of the envelope, her name and address typed across the front, *Western Union Telegram* stamped above. There was only one reason for this telegram.

Tears blurred her eyes and her nose began to run. Slipping a finger under the envelope flap, she pulled it open and slipped out the telegram. She unfolded it and read:

CASUALTY MESSAGE
TELEGRAM
THE SECRETARY OF WAR DESIRES ME TO EXPRESS
HIS DEEP REGRET
THAT YOUR
HUSBAND SERGEANT WILLIAM M OLOUGHLIN
HAS BEEN REPORTED MISSING IN ACTION SINCE
TWELVE JANUARY IN ITALY

Missing in action. She turned the phrase over and over in her mind, pretending that somehow, if she read the words differently, they could mean something else.

Missing in action didn't mean Bill was dead, just that the army couldn't find him.

Most certainly his plane had been shot down. Or maybe not. Maybe they crashed somewhere and got lost. Maybe bailed out over the sea and he was floating on a life raft with his buddies. That's happened. She had read such a story in a magazine.

Crazy ideas ricocheted through her mind.

Maybe the army had misplaced Bill. Somehow, among all the millions of men in uniform, what with the fighting and soldiers being moved back and forth across the globe, they had lost track of him. She wanted to imagine him on a lonely cot in an anonymous tent, somewhere in a forlorn army camp, wondering what the hell had happened to him.

Perhaps the army got frustrated trying to find him, and they had sent this telegram.

Once when she and Bill were together before he shipped out, she had asked him how the army kept track of so many soldiers. He explained that every morning in every military unit, at the beginning of the duty day, the soldiers stood in formation for roll call. If you weren't in formation, your first sergeant had to account for your whereabouts. Sick call. In the hospital. On furlough. In the stockade. At that exact time of the day, the army had to account for every warm body. So the chances that Bill had somehow gotten lost was not possible.

The other alternative was that he had run away, "gone over the hill," as the soldiers would say. In that case, he wouldn't be missing in action but a deserter and she wouldn't have received this telegram.

She blinked to force the tears from her eyes.

This was so unfair. Bill was a good man. They had plans. They had started a family. They represented what this world should be when this godforsaken war was over.

The room wobbled around her. Feeling dizzy, she closed her eyes to center herself. When she opened them, her vision remained blurred and the room continued to spin.

She felt suddenly brittle and collapsed against the floor. She lay in a heap, sobbing, filled with heartache and let the pain leak out the broken edges of her psyche.

Another voice pierced her misery. In her distorted mind she thought it was a siren, then realized the sound was too high-pitched. Maureen! Wailing from her crib.

Betty pushed up from the floor, sat, and let her gaze rove across the familiar surroundings. Everything about her life now seemed off kilter and forever skewed.

Maureen continued to wail.

Although Betty didn't like hearing her baby cry, the sound grounded her, reminding that there was something important and necessary beyond this wave of despair. She stood upright and shambled toward the bedroom, her gait becoming increasingly resolute the closer she approached the crib.

Maureen had kicked off her blanket and shrieked, her face beet red, her eyes clenched as tight as her tiny fists. Betty felt suddenly guilty for being a bad mother as if her distress was what caused the baby to cry.

Betty tucked the telegram into a skirt pocket and bundled Maureen in the blanket to carry back to the sofa. Settling onto the cushions, she rocked the baby in her arms and murmured soothing whispers. The baby kept wailing. Betty unbuttoned her blouse and began breastfeeding, the baby becoming instantly quiet.

She looked upon Maureen and thought, *Now you have no father. You never even set eyes on him.*

As Maureen nursed, Betty felt her sadness drain. Not much, but enough to bring clarity. She pondered what to do next. Unfortunately, it meant sharing this bad news and reliving the shock with every retelling.

When Maureen remained quiet, Betty buttoned up and made her way to the telephone. She couldn't keep this news from Bill's mother.

Eileen had rushed home on an extended lunch to take care of a business errand. After a quick bite of chicken salad spread on crackers, she was on her way to visit the Verwiels who lived in the basement apartment. The phone rang. Eileen kept still to hear who answered. Since her mother Florence and sister Patricia were home, one of them was closer to the phone.

The heavy footfalls meant Florence was going to answer. Eileen tilted her head to eavesdrop. She heard the plastic clatter of the receiver lifted off its hook, then her mother asking, "Hello, O'Loughlin residence."

A pause. Eileen piqued her ears.

Florence shrieked, then thumped to the floor. Eileen ran out the kitchen. Her mother lay crumpled on the floor, sobbing, still clutching the telephone.

Eyes swollen red and glassy with tears, she raised her face to Eileen. "Bill," she sobbed, "that was Betty. She just received a telegram. Bill is missing in action."

Heartbreak chopped through Eileen. All of her day's plans became abruptly trivial and vanished. She clutched her forehead, delirious with disbelief. Her brother, missing in action!

She perceived the evil shadow of war intruding into their home, bringing a despair that had darkened too many hearths and homes across this warring, suffering planet. Her mother lay on the floor, wailing as mothers had done since the beginning of humanity. Another sad mother lamenting the sad loss of a son in battle.

Eileen hurried toward her mother, took the phone and returned it to its cradle. Patricia had emerged from her bedroom, moonfaced with alarm. She stared at Florence, then at Eileen, her chin quivering. The two sisters and Florence collapsed into a ball, hugging, crying.

Eileen and her sisters—Marcelline, Florence, and Patricia—climbed out of the taxi in front of Betty's home on South Kingston Street and huddled to ward off the evening chill. Eileen broke loose from the group to bound up the stoop. She pushed the button for Betty's apartment. At the sound of the buzzer unlocking the door, they headed inside.

Shirley, Betty's sister, greeted them at the apartment door. Her expression was solemn, weighed by the sadness. Ruth took their coats.

Betty emerged from her bedroom and quietly shut that door behind her. Her eyes were bruised from the long hours of sorrow. At the sight of her, Eileen couldn't help but burst out crying, as did the other sisters. They clasped one another and sobbed, everyone sharing the feeling of being ripped open with anguish rushing into the void.

Betty retrieved the telegram from a secretary desk against the wall. Eileen took it first and read it, the words bringing a sour taste. She passed the telegram to Florence, who without reading it, quickly handed it to Patricia. With her husband Carl now in the army, Florence didn't want a foreshadowing of what her future might bring.

Ruth left for the kitchen to brew coffee. Marce had brought a bag with pastries, which she and Shirley arranged on a silver tray.

Betty sat on the middle cushion of the sofa, with Marce to her right, Patricia to her left. Eileen offered the armchair to Florence but she refused, preferring a plain chair in the corner.

"The baby?" Marce asked.

Betty blotted her nose with a kerchief. She cocked her head to the bedroom. "I just put her to bed."

"Ah," Marce replied, lowering her voice and nodding, but remaining quiet.

The sisters from the two families kneaded their kerchiefs and swiveled their gazes to Eileen, lifting their eyebrows hoping that she would carry the conversation.

Earlier, when she had been getting ready for this visit, Eileen had found a V-Mail she had written to Bill but never posted. The folded letter was in the top drawer of her dresser, where she kept her earrings and stationery. She had tucked it away, thinking she would mail it later, then decided otherwise because she wanted to amend the letter and dragged her feet about rewriting it.

Her gaze drifted to a wall calendar above the secretary desk. The month hadn't yet been changed to February. Her eyes zeroed in on January 12. Wednesday. Where had she been that day? The events flipped through her mind like she was shuffling snapshots. Typing reports. Sharing coffee with friends. Gossiping. Wondering what movie they should go see. Typical activities that now seemed so frivolous.

What time of the day had Bill gone missing in action? What had happened to him?

Shirley brought cups and saucers, which were balanced on knees. Ruth followed with the coffee pot and Shirley returned with the tray of pastries and napkins. All anyone managed to remark was a muted, "Thank you," to Ruth and Shirley as they made their rounds. Everyone nibbled on the pastries, and cups clinked when placed on the saucers.

Eileen wanted to suggest that they should congregate around the kitchen table. The collective grief brought a stuffiness that she knew wouldn't be relieved even if they opened a window. She had been to wakes before and eventually the mood lifted when people began swapping anecdotes about the departed. But Bill wasn't yet departed.

The most vexing and dismaying part of missing in action was that it was so open-ended. To hold a memorial service meant that you had given up hope. But when would you start to close the wound, let the heart start to heal? How long could you listen to the clock tick away the time, feeling the uncertainty nip away at your life?

Eileen wanted to ask Betty, *What's next?* But that was a silly question. The answer was, *Wait for more news from the War Department.*

Patricia fidgeted. She set her cup and saucer on an adjacent end table and began rifling through a stack of *LIFE* magazines on the bottom shelf. She placed one on her lap and thumbed the pages. Like every other periodical, most of the stories were about the war.

She lingered on a spread of a photo essay but from her angle, Eileen couldn't tell of what other than of soldiers doing soldier things.

"Do you know where in Italy Bill was?" Patricia asked without lifting her eyes from the magazine.

"No," Betty answered crisply. "You know the censors. In a letter he mentioned meatballs and spaghetti to indicate they were in Italy. But exactly where, I don't know."

She rose from the sofa, all eyes locking on her as if she was about to make a dramatic announcement. Instead, she walked to the secretary desk, opened a side drawer, and pulled out a stack of *National Geographic*. She returned to the sofa and unfolded the map tucked between the pages of the top magazine.

She spread the map across her lap. "This is of Africa. I used it to follow whatever news reports I managed to get. When Bill returned, I wanted him to show Maureen and me where he had been." She gathered the map and passed the magazine to Marce.

In her office at work, Eileen noted, they had similar maps tacked to the wall.

Betty opened the next magazines and unfolded the maps. "This is of the Mediterranean. This is one of Italy." She passed these along as well. Her expression indicated that with Bill missing in action her research had become a pointless exercise.

"Maybe he's in Switzerland," Patricia chimed in, her voice filled with naïve hope. "I've heard of damaged airplanes crash landing there. Maybe he got captured."

Florence clenched her jaw.

Eileen shot Patricia a pointed look, warning her to keep quiet. No doubt Betty had studied every possibility. Florence had as well, as had Eileen. What if Bill was a prisoner of war? How would the army know? If his airplane was shot down over enemy lines and he parachuted out, then how would the army know if he had been captured? Life as a prisoner of war, especially under the Germans, didn't seem like a friendly out-come. The Nazis tortured prisoners. But he might be alive.

Eileen studied her sister-in-law. Betty looked like a woman struggling to hold herself together. Eileen knew of other women who had lost a husband or a brother, an uncle, a cousin, a good friend, to this war. They were each of strong character, like Betty.

All Eileen and the others could do was weather this storm of heartache and pain and navigate toward the hope that Bill would reappear. And when the last of that hope faded like the rays of a setting sun, then it was time to accept the unacceptable and move on.

18

July 10, 1945

In the months since Bill had been reported missing, the arrival of official correspondence rekindled the hope of good news that he'd been found. Even learning that he was a POW would have brought solace that he was at least alive.

But every letter, every card, every sheet of mimeographed form confirmed to Betty that the worst had happened. The US Army bureaucracy cycled through its process, the various departments and offices grinding upon their red tape. Her husband as a living, breathing human being had entered the front of the machine, and these pieces of paper were what fell out the other end.

She'd requested from the army the home addresses of the three crewman she learned had survived that dreadful mission, Lieutenants Vincent, Haeberle, and Sergeant Franklin. She wrote to their families and asked if they could share any information about her missing husband.

Betty sorted through the day's mail and noted a letter from a F.W. Vincent. She opened the envelope and read this typewritten letter.

1st Lt. Fred W. Vincent
1812 N.W. Flanders
Portland, Oregon

July 5, 1945
Dear Mrs. O'Loughlin,
I am writing you with re to your late husband Sgt. William M. O'Loughlin.

I was Bill's pilot on the fatal mission of January 12th and have just returned to the states. I am taking this, the earliest opportunity, to write you and offer my sincerest regards to you.

We were bombing a dam just in back of the Cassino line. Bill was in the tail of the ship acting as rear gunner as well as engineer on this trip. The airplane was hit directly by flak and there was no opportunity to give any commands as the ship exploded into many parts.

Sgt. O'Loughlin had been with me on a number of previous missions. I held him in great respect both as a man and as a soldier. He was always ready to go on any mission regardless of the difficulties it presented. He was the type of man that any pilot would welcome on his crew. If there are any questions I could answer for you or any additional information or help in which

I could assist you in obtaining it would certainly be my pleasure to do so.

Please accept my most genuine condolences.

Sincerely yours,

Fred W. Vincent

❈ ❈ ❈

July 13, 1944

Betty finally received military correspondence that required her response, a form addressed from the Army Effects Bureau, File Number 61338-M, advising of her entitlement to Bill's death benefit and that they had received his personal effects.

She wrote back, using her given first name of "Ruth" instead of Betty:

7903 Kingston Ave.

Chicago, 17, Ill.

July 14, 1944

Army Effects Bureau

Kansas City Quartermaster Depot

Kansas City, 1 , Missouri

Attention: S.M. Greenstein

Capt. QMC

Dear Sir,

In reference to the personnel effects of my husband, Sgt. Wm. M. O'Loughlin, (serial number 20615746) your file number 61338-M, the following information is submitted for your approval.

I, Ruth E. O'Loughlin, being the lawfully wedded wife of Sgt. Wm. M. O'Loughlin, and the mother of our only child, Maureen Elizabeth age 11 mo. request and desire that you send all the personal property to me.

Although I have no written letter from my husband to substantiate my claim, it is my sincerest belief that he would unhesitatingly endorse such an action on your part.

Needless to say, I shall be more than willing to "receive receipt for, and, safely keep and store his property as a gratuitous bailee."

I believe this will answer all the information you requested.

Sincerely yours,

Ruth E. O'Loughlin

7903 Kingston Ave.

Chicago, 17, Ill.

August 6, 1945

A courier arrived at the house on Kingston Ave. He looked around fifty and wore a short gray jacket and matching cap that reminded Betty of a bus driver. Tucked under one arm, he carried a cardboard box, and in his other hand, he held a large envelope.

The box was labeled *Army Effects Bureau* and so must have contained Bill's personal belongings. She was surprised by the box's dimensions, 12 inches by 12 inches by 6 inches tall. It dismayed her that while Bill's memory loomed large in her conscious, his physical mementos could be contained in such a small box.

In the years following, Betty wouldn't remember much of this visit. The courier's face quickly faded into anonymity and his visit became lost in the blur of memories. She recalled that he smelled of cigarettes. Her mother had come out of her bedroom to greet the courier.

Betty recalled being polite and inviting him to set the box on the kitchen table where he first opened the envelope. He slipped out a sheaf of papers to include the bill of lading for the box and the inventory list for her signature. He used a pocket knife to cut the packing tape securing the box. She had felt a little numb as she watched the courier draw the items from the box and note them on the inventory sheet.

There were four columns: No. (number of items), Articles, No. (number of items), Articles. The courier read aloud the item description and quantity as he used a pencil to check them off the list.

"Cap. One." It was Bill's overseas cap, of olive drab wool.

"Stationery kit. One." A small flat box containing blank V-Mail stationery and envelopes.

"Shave brush. One." "Razors. Two." A pair of safety razors. "Hair brush. One." Army-issue with a wooden back. Betty took the brush and studied the thin strands of hair trapped in the bristles. This was all she had of Bill's body.

The courier continued the inventory. Military insignia. Three service ribbons. A pair of leather gloves. Wool scarf. Two GI issue web belts. Swim trunks. (In Italy during the middle of winter?) Shoulder patch of the Fifteenth Air Force. A broken string of rosary beads. Small wooden crucifix. His leather billfold. Empty save for some tattered cards.

The item that most captured Betty's interest was a small picture frame holding the photo on their wedding day. The happiness of that moment bloomed bright. There was no way then they could've predicted this bitter outcome.

Betty took the picture and stared. Her eyes glossed over with tears. Betty put her arm on her mom's shoulder and gave a squeeze.

The courier acted as if he hadn't seen this poignant display. He returned everything to the box and turned the inventory for Betty's attention. She filled out the bottom of the form, signing as the bailee. Her mother signed as witness.

The courier lifted from his seat at the table. Reliving the scene, Betty couldn't remember if she or her mom had let the man out. What remained in her memory was the emptiness that small cardboard box had brought to her, a reminder that her husband was gone forever.

August 30, 1945
Betty received a second letter from another crewmember on Bill's airplane, addressed in a loopy scrawl. Dated August 24, return address of Clearwater, Kansas.

Unlike Vincent's letter, this was handwritten in pen, the loose cursive script spread across four pages of stationery.

July 13, 1945

Dear Mrs. O'Loughlin,

I intended to write you long ago, but I guess I've been enjoying my furlough too much. I'll try and tell you about the mission that we went down as I remember it.

We were hit by flak after we left the target. It was a direct hit and the plane was set on fire and we were completely out of control. The right wing was shot off I heard later. I was knocked unconscious temporarily so I really do not know. When I came to, the plane was upside down with fire burning in the cockpit. I escaped by unfastening my safety belt and falling through a large hole blown in the top of the cockpit. I believe Lt. Vincent was still there when I left. He said he was blown out of the plane by another explosion. Probably the gas tanks. I was captured when I got to the ground and taken to a hospital and later to a prison camp. I thought I was the only survivor of the crew until I met Lt. Vincent at Barth. I later found out that the bombardier, Wille Franklin, had also gotten out. All the other men in the front of the plane got out. The ones in the back went down with the plane. Everything happened so fast and in such a state of confusion that it is really hard to tell just what did happen.

I did not know your husband very well. They change crews around so much that lots of time we didn't have much of a chance to get acquainted. The only two that I really knew well were Sgt. Schroder, the top turret gunner, and Lt. Vincent.

I'm sorry the rest of the crew were not as fortunate as the ones that escaped. It might have been just the other way around if we had been hit in another place. I'm sure that there was nothing we could do to help them, though. Everything happened so fast.

I want to thank you for writing to my mother. She has certainly enjoyed hearing from you. I believe the war is harder for the people at home than for the soldiers themselves.

Sincerely yours,

1st Lt. John Haeberle

September 24, 1945

Betty received a letter from a surprising source, Joe Parisi, whom she recalled was Bill's friend from their wedding in

Charleston. He wrote to express his condolences about Bill and that upon being mustered out of the army, he was returning to Chicago. He wondered if it would be appropriate if he stopped by to say hello.

She barely remembered him. August 1942 was a while back and they hadn't kept in touch. His image coalesced in her mind. Lots of hair. A thin mustache.

Betty showed the letter to her mother.

She asked, "What's he like?"

"Serious. Not a jokester like Bill."

"What's he look like?"

"Nice enough. Not as tall. Good hair. Well-groomed as they say."

Her mother flipped the letter over to reread it. "What do you think he wants?"

"Like he said, a visit."

Her mom glanced at baby Maureen, now a toddler. "Tell him you have a daughter. Have him make up his mind beforehand."

Betty knew what her mother meant. If Joe had any romantic intentions, then Maureen had to figure into his plans. Some men aren't welcoming to children who weren't theirs.

When she wrote back, Betty had much to sort through. People assumed that with the end of the war, things would go back to normal and wartime anxieties would evaporate.

However, that wasn't the case. Many of the old worries simply became new worries while other old worries remained the same. During the war, work had been plentiful but the return of peace brought a double whammy.

First, since war material was no longer needed, the factories were shut down. Sometimes the announcements came at mid-shift.

The second whammy was that returning GIs expected to walk back into their old jobs, if those still existed. Female workers were immediately displaced, to resume their roles as homemakers and mothers-to-be.

And like tens of thousands of other women, Betty found herself as a war widow. The loss of Bill O'Loughlin still burned, leaving a large void in her heart. But she had to move on, to provide for Maureen and for herself.

When she received Joe's letter, she was well aware of the subtext. What she most remembered about him, ironically enough, was that incident during the wedding. Joe didn't hide his displeasure that Bill had borrowed, without asking, his army shoes.

On their first "date," Joe wore his Army Air Force uniform, its upper sleeves resplendent with the stripes of a sergeant first class. Sewn above his left breast pocket, he brandished the Honorable Discharge Eagle, what veterans called the Ruptured Duck. During their time together, he was charming, making Betty feel special.

The courtship was short and matter-of-fact. With Bill, she felt as if fate had brought them together, and his unfortunate passing seemed like a mistake. Things between them looked so perfect. With Joe Parisi, it was as if fate was trying to make amends for taking Bill. *This is not what you wanted but is the best I can do.* Their arrangement seemed like another mix-and-match between all the returning vets and the broken-hearted widows.

They were married at Saint Brides Church in Chicago. Betty noticed that although Joe was dressed in a civilian suit, he wore brown army-issue oxfords. Without asking, she knew these were the same pair of shoes Bill had borrowed for their marriage ceremony. Here she was ready to start a fresh chapter of her life with a new husband and looking down at Joe's shoes, she was saddened to be reminded of Bill and their wedding day. The irony spun in Betty's mind. *Joe, even though you're a good man and wearing your own shoes, you'll never fill them like Bill had.*

March 9, 1947
Shortly after six this evening, Joe entered the front door of their home, a comfortable-enough, one-story house on East End Ave. He worked as a photo engraver. Betty rushed to greet him as he expected.

When he hung his coat on the hook by the front door, he sniffed, turned about, sniffed again. "What happened to dinner?"

"It'll be a little late. I just put the chicken in the oven."

Joe made a show of looking at his watch.

"I'm sorry," she replied. "Running errands took longer than expected."

As she readied dinner, she heard the water run in the bathroom. When he returned, he had changed into his casual clothes, which she had neatly pressed. He took the day's newspaper into the living room to plant himself in an armchair, read, and smoke a cigarette.

Dinner was the usual. Quiet. Nothing said to Maureen and she said nothing to him. He never mistreated her, either, for the record. Only that he showed her the barest of attention and when he did, it was cool at most. Joe didn't act bothered that Maureen ignored him in return. In fact, he acted as if he preferred that arrangement.

After Betty collected the dishes, he'd return to his armchair in the living room, click on the radio, light a cigarette, and lose himself again in the newspaper.

When the dishes were washed, rinsed, and stacked in the drying rack, the kitchen table wiped, and the leftovers covered with foil and stowed in the refrigerator, Betty removed her apron and walked toward the piano in the living room. She sat on the bench, ran her fingers along the keys to warm up, and began to play, "Together." As the melody sprang from the piano, she sang the lyrics.

Maureen sat nearby on the carpet and watched.

Betty looked at her daughter and wondered how different life would be for the both of them had Bill survived.

19

Mrs. Ruth E. O'Loughlin.   20 November 1947
7226 Cornell Avenue
Chicago 49, Illinois

*D*ear Mrs. O'Loughlin,
The Department of the Army desires that you be furnished information concerning the resting place of your husband, the late Sergeant William M. O'Loughlin, A.S.W. 20 615 746.

With deep regret I must inform you that, although the records of his office disclose that the remains of your husband were reverently interred, it was not possible, because of the manner in which he met his death, to identify his remains individually.

The remains of your loved one and other fallen comrades are currently resting as a group in United States Military Cemetery Marzanello Nuovo, located approximately nineteen miles southeast of Cassino, Italy.

The American Graves Registration Service exhausts every possible clue which might lead to individual identification of

United States deceased personnel; however, if further research fails to establish their individual identity, the remains of this group will be returned to the United States for final interment in a national cemetery designated by The Quartermaster General. All legal next of kin will be advised at a later date of the national cemetery in which final interment will be made and will also be notified of the time of burial.

May I extend my sincerest sympathy in your great loss.

Sincerely yours,

THOMAS B. LARKIN
Major General
The Quartermaster General

Maureen bumped against the kitchen table, startling Betty.

"Mom, what are you reading?" Maureen asked. "You look sad."

Betty put the letter aside. She decided not to say that it was about Bill because she didn't want to explain, as she did with every piece of army correspondence, that *it was about your dead father.* She brightened her expression and answered, "It's from the government," hoping that Maureen hadn't yet connected that "from the government" meant "it's about your father."

"Joe will be home soon," Betty said, referring to her husband, Maureen's stepfather. "Why don't do you go back to your room and I'll call you for dinner. Look at one of your picture books."

Maureen wandered out of the kitchen, leaving Betty to circle her thoughts back to the letter and what to think about Bill. Previous correspondence listed him as *Killed In Action*, placed of death—*Mediterranean Area*, ending the speculation that he was no longer *Missing In Action*. The purpose for this *drip, drip, drip* of information was that it demonstrated how the army bureaucracy churned along, following its rules, paperwork winding through labyrinths of corridors. To its credit, the government was making a good effort at bringing home all of its "honored dead," at least those it could find. How many lay at the bottom of the oceans?

This letter she would add to her box of documents sent to her concerning Bill. They were mostly administrative forms dealing with his assignments and transfers, the dates he'd gone on sick call, another inventory of his personal effects. Routine matters. She got the impression she'd received some of the papers by mistake when there was no accompanying cover letter. Her address would appear on a form that she was to be notified as his next of kin, which had already happened. She imagined a harried clerk shuffling through Bill's personnel file, collected these documents—overwhelmed by the avalanche of papers on his desk and spotting her name—slipped them into an envelope and sent the packet her way.

The documents were an illuminating peek at the workings inside the army with stamped areas for signatures and stamped meter dates indicting when the individual forms arrived on a particular desk and another stamp indicating when it was passed on. As she read the dates, she noted where she had been at the time, two parallel worlds ticking away.

One detail did stand out: the mention of where Bill was buried overseas. The United States Military Cemetery, Marzanello Nuovo, Italy. Plot C, Row 12, Grave 134, 135, 136, 137.

Army correspondence kept repeating the need for a group burial and here they listed four graves. Obviously, one for each of the men trapped inside the doomed B-25: Sgt. William O'Loughlin, S. Sgt. Donald Davis, S. Sgt. Harold Shrader, and Sgt. Leo P. Hassett.

Betty pondered the macabre details of digging the remains from the wreckage of the *Buckeye Cannon Ball*, where the dead crew had been left rotting for months in the Italian countryside while the war raged around them. The bodies must've been heaped together in a big mess if the army couldn't separate the corpses into individual graves.

The thoughts transported Betty into an odd place, where Bill as her husband, Bill as the father of her child, existed alongside this other Bill who lay as a jumble of broken bones with his dead comrades. One Bill walked and smoked, smiling effortlessly with the confidence that a prosperous and shining future lay before him. The other Bill remained still and curled in a stiff ball, buried in the ground, a casualty of war.

Betty reflected on the army's wording of Bill and his comrades: *the honored dead?*

But what about the honored living? The survivors who did what they were asked? The survivors like herself who had sacrificed their true love? What about survivors like Maureen who had sacrificed a father they never met? Where was the packet of correspondence detailing how they were to handle surviving?

In idle moments, Betty juggled her many questions. For answers, she could've turned to the parish priest. Or to her mother-in-law, Florence, who had lost her only son. Or to Bill's sister, Florence, and the O'Loughlin siblings who had lost their only brother. But what could anyone say?

There was only one response. Push the grief down and move on. The more you brought the grief to the surface, it didn't wilt and die. Rather, it flourished like a weed. Soon you'd be choking on the grief the way a garden chokes on weeds.

"What do you have there?" It was her husband, Joe.

Betty tucked the papers back into the envelope. She hadn't heard Joe enter and wished she had. He got edgy whenever she concerned herself with matters about Bill. He never uttered any overt words of jealousy but the sentiment was there.

Joe leaned over the table and glanced at the envelope. The Army Quartermaster return address was enough to verify what this about.

"What's it been?" he asked, "three years?" Meaning three years since Bill was killed.

He didn't press Betty for an answer. Not that he wanted one. The question was his way of voicing his resentment.

Joe left the kitchen. The radio in the living room clicked on, followed by the murmur of a song. She detected the whiff of burning sulfur from a lit match and heard the rustle of a newspaper. At least Joe was giving her this time to be alone.

Betty shoved the envelope into a stack of correspondence on the secretary desk. She returned to the kitchen, slipped an apron over her head, and tied the strings. Using a voice loud enough to be heard in the living room, she announced, "I'm making pork chops. Fried potatoes. That okay?"

"That's fine."

From the ice box, she set out the dish with the pork chops she had seasoned earlier and another dish with sliced potatoes. She placed a frying pan on the stove, poured oil in the pan, and lit the burner. So this was what moving on felt like.

DEPARTMENT OF THE ARMY
Office of the Quarter General
Washington 25 D. C.
IN REPLY REFER TO BURIAL OF
Sgt. William M. O'Loughlin, 20 615 74611   *May 1948*
United States Military Cemetery
Marzanello Nuova, Italy

Mrs. Ruth E. O'Loughlin
7226 Cornell Avenue
Chicago 49, Illinois

> *Dear Mrs. O'Loughlin,*
> *The Department of the Army desires that you be given the latest information regarding the disposition of the remains of your husband, the late Sergeant William M. O'Loughlin, A.S.N. 20 615 746. In view of the circumstances of his death, which also caused the death of three of his comrades, it has not been possible to establish individual identification. Accordingly, these honored dead have been temporarily interred as a group in the United States Military Cemetery Marzanello Nuova, Italy, pending their return to this country for final burial.*
> *The remains represented in this group will be returned simultaneously to the United States within the next few months for final burial in:*
> *Fort Scott National Cemetery, Fort Scott, Kansas*

The plan for the disposition of groups, with respect to which only the collective identity is known, is in keeping with the provisions of Public Law 383, 79th Congress, as amended by Section 3, Public Law 368, 80th Congress. We believe you will agree that the burial of this group of honored dead in one of our national shrines, where perpetual care can be given their graves, is both fitting and proper.

It is vitally essential that you promptly inform the Commanding Officer, Quartermaster Depot, Attention AGRD, 601 Hardesty Avenue, Kansas City 1, Missouri, of any change in your address. If you fail to do this, it may not be possible to contact you when the remains reach the United States and to notify you the date final interment will be effected.

In due course, the Superintendent of above National Cemetery will communicate with you with regard to burial arrangements. Information as to time of interment will be furnished sufficiently in advance to afford attendance by you and other members of your family desiring to participate.

Please accept my sincere sympathy in your great loss.

Sincerely yours,

G. A. Horkan
Major General, QMC
Chief, Memorial Division

November 13, 1950

When Betty received the notice of Bill's final interment, she would have wanted to discuss the matter with Florence, Bill's mother, but she had passed away suddenly last July. So, Betty decided to talk about the matter with her sister-in-law, Florence. They'd become close friends and a shoulder for the other to lean on in tough times. This was such an occasion and so Betty arrived at Florence's home.

When had the army first alerted Betty of their plans to reinter Bill in the US? Two years ago? Betty tempered her dismissal of the army's glacial pace in this matter as Bill was no doubt one of hundreds of thousands of fallen men who had to be accounted for, re-buried, and have a grave marker made.

This recent letter was dated the eighth of this month and signed by Major F.A. Kirk, Quartermaster General, Memorial Division. After all the army's previous and lengthy correspondence notifying Betty about the disposition of Bill and the administrative logistics of moving his remains from Italy to final burial in the US, this letter was surprisingly brief. Bill and his fellow aircrewmen had been buried in Grave No. 1780, Section 2, at the Fort Scott National Cemetery, Fort Scott, Kansas. Included in the letter were two black and white snapshots of the grave marker—a white marble slab engraved with the names of Staff Sergeants Davis and Schrader on top, Sergeants O'Loughlin and Hassett in the middle, and Air Corps along the bottom. In the background, rows and rows of white markers stretched past the edges of the photo.

Since Betty had arrived late in the day, Carl was home from work. He greeted her at the door and welcomed her in. Betty shared the army's letter with Florence and Carl, who re-read it several times.

While Carl brewed coffee, Florence rummaged in a cabinet drawer and withdrew a road map. She unfolded it on the dining table and spun it to orient herself. After finding Illinois, she circled a finger to locate Fort Scott, Kansas, and traced her finger back to Chicago.

"It's a good eight hours to Kansas City," she said, "and I guess Fort Scott is an hour past that."

Nine hours one way, Betty thought. *And nine hours back.* Not counting time waiting for the bus or train. The two days traveling would bookend a day spent at the cemetery. What else could they do at Fort Scott besides look at graves?

She regarded Florence and Carl. Both bore an expression that told Betty the decision to go would be up to her but that they would gladly accompany her.

Three days away from home. What to do with Maureen? If they took her, that was an extra round trip ticket. They couldn't leave her at home, not with Joe working. All of Bill's other sisters worked or had families of their own to watch so it would be a big imposition asking them to mind Maureen.

Carl poured himself a cup of coffee and leaned against the kitchen counter. His gaze was on the floor, lost in thought.

Betty returned to her musings.

And after all that expense, what would they gain? How long would it take to acknowledge the grave marker and what was on it? What would the effort serve? It would provoke no new memories. In fact, a visit to the grave would rekindle more grief and regrets over what might have been.

Betty said, "I don't see the point."

Carl was looking her. He never talked about his experience in the war. Because of his German background he'd been sent to the Pacific and—irony of ironies—while Bill served in the Army Air Force, Carl was in the Anti-Aircraft Artillery. Florence related that his unit had been assigned to an infantry division and took part in the invasion of Luzon. The fighting had been grueling, some of the worst of the war. Carl came back in one piece, fortunately, but many of his buddies hadn't, and in quiet moments, it was obvious that he still carried that burden.

Betty felt the need to explain herself. She said, "I lost my husband."

Florence replied, "And I lost my brother."

"And I," Carl broke his silence, "lost my best friend."

The moment hung heavy above them. They looked at one another and released their anxiety with a collect sigh.

With little ceremony, Florence folded the map and returned it to the drawer. She took one of the photos and inserted the other with the letter into its envelope. "Here." She handed the envelope to Betty.

In a way, Bill had been returned to them, partially at least. He was in his final resting place. As far as the army was concerned, their file on William M. O'Loughlin, Sergeant, 12th Army Air Force, was closed.

There were no more details to consider.

Betty glanced to the entrance. She had a fleeting image of Bill walking into the apartment, his abrupt appearance showing that this entire episode had been one long nightmare.

She blinked. There was nothing but the door and the realization that Bill was gone forever.

20

August 2016

M y Aunt Kathleen, one of Bill's nieces born just before he died, and her husband, John Hamilton, were on vacation in Italy and had spent the night in the picturesque seaport of Gaeta. This trip was, in part, to fulfill a childhood dream, in which she saw herself finding a tree marking the spot where Bill's airplane had crashed. She had brought along a GPS to locate the coordinates of the crash site as provided by army records: 41 degrees 32 minutes north, 13 degrees 52 minutes east.

They hired Rosario, a local taxi driver, for their trek into the Italian countryside. Although Rosario advertised himself as fluent in English, that turned out not to be the case. Then in serendipity—one of many instances of serendipity and coincidences that day—Kathleen met a young man named Nicola outside their hotel who had recently returned from his university studies in the US. As expected, he was quite fluent in English and agreed to be hired as their translator for the day.

The distance the crow flies from Gaeta to the coordinates of Bill's plane was about twenty-five miles, which doesn't seem far until you drive those narrow, twisting mountain roads. Even with the GPS, Kathleen, John, and crew had a hell of a time keeping their bearings in the rugged terrain overgrown with thick vegetation.

They managed to find the Isoletta Dam on the Liri River, whose attempted destruction on that ill-fated day in 1944 cost Bill his life. The dam remains today in almost the same condition it had been during the war. An austere and unassuming structure, its concrete was weathered by the passing decades and coated by a veneer of slick, green moss. Given its bucolic appearance and surprisingly modest size, it was hard to believe this dam had once been the focus of so much attention during the war, both to defend and to destroy it.

From Isoletta, the crash-site coordinates lay northeast, consistent with the documented events of the day since Bill's B-25 was heading in that direction when it had been shot down after bombing the dam.

Continuing to search for the bomber's crash site, Kathleen stopped and asked a farmer for directions. He lit up with enthusiasm and directed them to the nearby village of Falveterra where they would find Floriano Bertoni, a birder who during a hike through the hills, had found a part of a downed American aircraft from the war. Once in Falveterra, word of the visiting Americans spread throughout the village and Rosario's little taxi was mobbed by the locals. The scene seemed straight out of a movie, the Italians bubbling with cheer and a hearty welcome.

The mayor was immediately summoned to greet the adventuresome American tourists. He'd been out jogging and was brought forward, still in his stylish track suit. In short order, they were introduced to the nephew of a local writer, Adriano Piccirilli, who'd authored a history of the air war over Italy and had cataloged many of the aircraft lost in the area.

Floriano Bertoni came forward to declare that yes, he had found debris at those coordinates and turned it over to a neighbor who collected and preserved such wreckage as tribute to the sacrifices of the Americans who had liberated the village from the Germans. Though the war had ended more than 70 years ago, vivid memories were handed down from generation to generation of the brutal German occupation and the bitter campaign to oust them from the country. All the locals bubbled with appreciation for what the Americans had done.

Kathleen and the others drove to the villa where aircraft wreckage was stored and the parts reassembled as best as possible. By referring to the coordinates of where Bill's plane had gone down, the villa owner's son came forward with an aluminum piece about 24 inches long by 12 inches wide, a section of the lower fuselage belonging to the *Buckeye Cannon Ball*, tail number 41-13210. Tangible proof that Bill had been here.

For Kathleen, holding this battered piece of aluminum brought a sense of completion. Of course, it had been naïve to expect to find the imagined tree from her childhood. And Bill's remains had long since been recovered and interred at the Fort Scott National Cemetery.

The moment was not bittersweet as she expected, but one of finality, even a bit of unexplained joy. Though there had been no mystery of what had happened to Bill, the discovery of this part of his doomed aircraft tangibly documented the final chapter of his life.

But not quite.

June 2017

As a writer and novelist in his later years, my father Joseph, Kathleen's oldest brother, had begun collecting material about Uncle Bill in the hopes of penning his biography. He had visited Bill's daughter, Maureen, who lived in Alabama at the time, in order to interview her regarding her recollections after the war. Maureen had given him files with many of the original documents and keepsakes that her mother

Betty had kept regarding the husband she had lost. To continue his research, in 2015, my father had submitted an additional FOIA request to the US Army for their wartime records about Bill. He continued his quest to document his uncle's life but was troubled on what direction to take the manuscript. He and I discussed several angles he could take on the story but he still harbored his misgivings.

In early June 2017, my father drove to visit his sister Pudy at her home in Milpitas, and left his Jeep Grand Cherokee at her place while he flew from San Jose to Riverside to visit with their other siblings. Sadly, my father died unexpectedly during that trip on June 12.

Following my father's death, I was inventorying his estate and the one item I couldn't find was the folder with the files about Bill that Maureen had given him. It seemed that this effort to chronicle Bill's life had come to a frustrating end.

Two months passed and the family decided to gift my father's Jeep Grand Cherokee to a nephew. He and I went to pick up the Jeep at Pudy's house. While in the process of cleaning it out, incredibly, we found the missing folders. It was as if Bill had somehow willed that his story would remain safe in the most unlikely of places. My aunts and uncles decided that I was the one to finish writing Bill's biography. At first, I refused since I am a hydrogeologist and a technical writer. I felt I was not gifted with the creative writing skills needed to do Bill's story justice. I contacted Maureen via the internet to let her know that I had the files and but was hoping I could keep them for a time while I ruminated on what to do.

Roughly a year later, my Aunt Judy called, asking about the files and my progress in completing the biography. The reason for her call was to let me know that Maureen was trying to track me down in hopes of obtaining the original documents as they were the only keepsakes of her father. To my horror, I could not locate the folder. All I could think was that I must have left it in a hotel room during one of several business trips, when I used to read it in my down time.

Desperate, I retraced my steps and called every hotel I'd stayed at—in Oregon, Arizona, Minnesota—hoping that someone had turned it in. But no one had, and I was told, that after 90 days, the hotel clears out the lost and found. Hoping that the folder might still be in my home, I offered my kids the lofty sum of a one-hundred-dollar reward to whoever found it. We turned our house over seven ways to Sunday but nothing.

Reluctantly, I called Maureen about what had happened. She said to forget about it and reassured me that the files would eventually turn up. But I could not! I lost sleep wondering where the folder had gone. In fact, on several occasions, I'd wake up in the middle of the night with an epiphany about the folder's location. I would leap out of bed to verify my thought, to no avail. It was driving me mad.

I called Maureen again to tell her that I was afraid that the folder would never be found. This time she wasn't as forgiving. Actually, she was quite forceful and implied that her son (Bill's grandson), a former Marine, might just get on an airplane and fly out to "help me find it."

Without the files, I set aside any plans for completing the book.

Several months went by and through my Aunt Judy I learned that my Uncle Billy—the one named for Bill O'Loughlin and who was born just days before his death (see January10 and worry for his sister Marce)—had lapsed into a coma and that his end was near. I reassured my aunt that I would attend the funeral when the time came. As I sat in a chair to process this news, my daughter, Gabbie, entered the kitchen and asked, "Dad, do you remember that big file you've been looking for? You know, the one you promised me a hundred dollars if I found it?"

My moods shifted from sad to surprised. "Yeah?"

She pointed in the direction to her bedroom. "Well, you owe me that money. It's sitting on my dresser right now."

I jumped from the chair. "What?"

"The folder has notes and writing all over it, doesn't it?"

I hustled to her bedroom and there it was, complete with photographs, original letters from the surviving crew of the Buckeye, among many other keepsakes. A chill ran through my entire body. There is no explanation for how the file got there.

As if to add to the mystery, within a few hours, my Uncle Bill (Bill O'Loughlin's namesake) died.

Several days later, I attended Uncle Billy's funeral and when I returned home, there was a cardboard envelope addressed to my father from the US Army Human Resources Command waiting on the doorstep. It contained a CD with the personnel and unit files my father had requested from the army way back in 2015, four years prior. The information on the disk filled in the many gaps my father was struggling with while trying to pen Bill's story and has largely formed the basis of this book. There was also a formal apology from the US Army for the delay in getting the requested materials as they were reorganizing their filing system.

All my life, I've been struck by incidents of synchronicity and serendipity that couldn't have been mere chance. The instances described here are but just a few of *many* regarding Bill O'Loughlin's story, and I can't shake the feeling that Bill has reached from the past and tapped me to bring his story to a close. I struggle with why!

The writers I found who helped me draft the manuscript also brought their own share of startling coincidences that aligned with the saga of Bill's life. To be frank, the writers who helped me in this project were the very first I called and interviewed. Yes, I made one phone call and took a huge gamble. The circumstances of that first conversation with Mark and Mario are yet another strange set of oddities.

To my surprise, Mario was quite familiar with the Italian campaign in World War II and even knew about the Isoletta Dam. As chance would have it, Mario was an army aviator and flew Cobras. In an advanced aviation course, his primary thesis was a discourse on the disastrous attack over the Rapido River by the 36ᵗʰ Division and the need to destroy the Isoletta Dam. He later related an even more amazing detail. One of his clients from another project had worked at the North American Plant in Inglewood making B-25s at the very same time Bill O'Loughlin was stationed there. The two might have crossed paths or even met. But the cosmic alignment didn't end there. The very day that the client was drafted into military service was the very same day Bill was shot down and killed. I believe there is more to this story but I think I will leave that up to Bill.

What to make of Bill O'Loughlin? His loss was but one of the more than 600,000 Americans who gave up their lives during World War II. Trying to make sense of who Uncle Bill was became a journey of profound illumination and appreciation. He lived in a different time obviously, but the concerns and reactions of people back then were no different than what ours would've been.

In piecing together Bill and Betty's life, I tried to imagine what it was like stepping out onto those cold Chicago streets to eavesdrop on their conversations. Some details stood out. Seems everybody smoked. Everybody liked a beverage. Unlike in today's ultra-casual environment, people back then dressed up as a matter of course. In researching the menus, everybody enjoyed a good meal, one that would satisfy any modern foodie.

While I was aware of how important America's industrial output had been, the enormity of our nation's war effort astonished me. Seemingly overnight, gigantic factories and military bases the size of towns sprang from empty ground. The countryside became dotted with airfields, all of them buzzing with squadrons of warplanes, their crews honing skills for inevitable combat.

America's Arsenal for Democracy was colossal in scale. However, for much of the war, the grim arithmetic was to build ships, tanks, and airplanes faster than the enemy could destroy them. But that advantage in material would not have made a difference if we did not have men who advanced into harm's way to punish the enemy.

The Germans and the Japanese did not simply yield from conquered territory. They were driven out. Every bomb, every machine gun bullet, that sprang from Uncle Bill's bomber and found its mark, was but another nail in the coffin of our enemies.

My research revealed interesting details about how the war was fought. I'd never given much thought on how the Army

Air Force arrived in North Africa, thinking that it had deployed from England to support the landings at Casablanca. The truth was, the bulk of American air power sent to Europe actually came by way of the British Gold Coast, modern day Ghana. The B-25s of the 321st Bombardment Group began leapfrogging from makeshift airfields laid across the swamps of southern Florida and Louisiana, then hop-scotched to Puerto Rico, to Belize, to Brazil, before winging to Ascension Island and then Accra. The ground-support elements sailed across the Atlantic for Accra and from there journeyed north to Algeria . . . by train! Who knew? This was so much forgotten history.

Moreover, Uncle Bill's story overlapped with two of the great works of American literature, *Catch-22* by Joseph Heller, and *A Canticle for Liebowitz* by Walter M. Miller Jr. The connection is that both Heller and Miller fought in World War II as crewmen aboard B-25s with the 15th Air Force in Italy; Miller, coincidentally, was also a tail gunner like Bill. While *Catch-22* is an acclaimed satire of war and bureaucracy, in researching the history of the 447th Bomber Squadron, there wasn't much to laugh at. Heller admitted that his experience was mostly "milk runs," while Bill's unit flew into the teeth of German fighters and antiaircraft guns. Miller's take on the tragedy of war shows through his novel and he suffered with PTSD that he could never overcome. Had Bill survived the war, perhaps he too would've chronicled his service into a bestseller.

The great crusade to save democracy and defeat fascism was not decided by the lofty pronouncements of politicians and generals, but by men like my uncle, Sergeant William M. O'Loughlin, who carried out their assignments with diligence and dedication. They didn't regard themselves as heroes, just ordinary soldiers with a job to do.

Even years after Uncle Bill's death, his loss rippled through my family. His daughter, Maureen, wondered every day how different her life would've been had she known her father. And there is no doubt that Bill remained the light of Betty's life. For the Verwiels, Uncle Bill's tragic death seemed too unfathomable for comprehension, and so he remained a venerated, though silent, presence. But his full story had been lost to time and to the silence that grief sometimes brings.

Then the universe decided that at last, Uncle Bill's odyssey from uncertain civilian to fallen soldier needed to be told and that responsibility apparently fell upon me. Collecting all the strands of Bill's life and braiding them into a complete story seemed an overwhelming task, but Bill's spirit nudged me forward, educating me, enlightening me, and guiding me to the right people until I think I've presented here not just the retelling of a portion of Sergeant William M. O'Loughlin's life, but an inspiring homage to the men and women of the Greatest Generation.

Acknowledgments

I am not a creative writer. I've never had a clear idea what it takes to put a book together, particularly one of this nature. I have always been impressed with my brother Chris and my Father with their ability to sit and simply "let it flow." This accounting of my great Uncle Bill and his family and friends is a bit different in that it is a conglomeration of dog-eared personal letters, military documents, detailed history, word of mouth, and stories I remember from my youth. There were moments that needed filling and in doing so, creative license ruled the day. I think I've gotten it right but it would not have been completed without the help of many.

I have to start by thanking my awesome, beautiful, funny, and supportive wife Ann and our two children, Jake and Gabbie. From reading early drafts to giving advice on particular events all the way through cover design, they were as important to getting this completed as I was. Jake unknowingly provided inspiration to me when he submitted a shortened version of the story to his AP English class during his junior year of high school. And providentially, Gabbie found the "missing" file of pictures and letters, which I took as a sign to get busy. Ann gave early feedback on tone of the book, which made a big difference, and she helped immensely, pouring over early 1940's letters covered with smudged, faded, and worn cursive writing.

To everyone at Mark Graham Communications, Graham Publishing Group, and in particular, Mario Acevedo. I thought I knew a lot about World War II until I met Mario. His knowledge of the Army Air Force's efforts to support ground troops up the boot of Italy is staggering. Further, his ability to simplify military history, detailed combat situations, and complex machines is mind numbing. He is like some sort of a freakish stenographer with a photographic memory. He never missed a detail.

To Maureen O'Loughlin Hay Adams (Bill's daughter)... We did it! This would never had happened without your insights. Thanks for taking my calls! Thanks for walking me through your mom's recollections. And most importantly, thanks for sharing your life without your dad. I can't imagine.

To my Aunt Marcelline (Pudy) Cruzen for her early edits and for her recollections of Bill and his family, including my grandparents (Marcelline and John Verwiel) in the early 1940s. Although not prominent figure in the book, they are all responsible for filling in a lot of gaps in my knowledge of family history.

To Kathleen and John Hamilton. The next time you two go on vacation I would like to go with you; I'll even carry your bags, if necessary. Kathy was the most vocal person imploring that I complete the journey of this book. Although she didn't know how the book would turn out, she knew there was something there. She is not one to take no for an answer, and apparently she was right!

To Kathleen Ladwig Lilley for her recollections on her mom and dad (Florence and Carl). I recall growing up with my dad telling me that Carl fought in the war, but it was probably not a comfortable topic to bring up. Although not detailed in this story, Carl fought in some of the most brutal battles in the Pacific Theatre of WWII, even receiving a commendation from none other than General Douglass MacArthur for his efforts on Corregidor. Perhaps there's another book in the making.

To Vicki V. Howland and Fred Vincent IV, children of the Buckeye Cannonball pilot Fred Vincent. Fred kept a diary while in a German prison Camp, which provided the details of the Buckeye Cannonball's last mission, from flight prep to getting hit by flak over Isoletta Dam.

To Christian Colline, a work friend, for starting me on the road to discovery with his help researching Bill and Carl's military records.

To Lieutenant Colonel John Verwiel (r) for his assistance in obtaining Bill O'Loughlin's early military records and for encouraging my dad to continue the search for information.

To Dan Davis, Jim Cetrullo, and Dan Verwiel (brother) for their final edits on select portions of the manuscript. To Louis Bull for his special brand of encouragement and for his stories of his own father's experiences in WWII.

To Bill Holbrow (my Brother-in-Law) for the contracts and legal support. Blah...Blah....Blah...I'm Glad you like that stuff.

To Patricia A. Verwiel, my mom, for her ancestry research in the early stages of the book, for her suggestions on content, and for her support in keeping this book going.

And last but not least, to my dad, Joseph William Verwiel, for the obvious reasons. I hope this book was completed the way you wanted it.

Made in the USA
Coppell, TX
13 June 2021

57369430R00166